HOW TO BE A ROCK STAR

By the Fleetwood Mac guitarist who got away,
dated a supermodel, played with Ray Davies,
Rod Stewart, Jeff Beck, Peter Green and Cat Stevens,
made superstars of The Sex Pistols, Duran Duran and
The Pet Shop Boys, and lived to tell the tale.

DAVID AMBROSE

WITH LESLEY-ANN JONES

Little Wing

First edition published 2020

ISBN: 978-1-911273-92-9 (hardcover)

All images are from the authors' collection unless otherwise stated.

Published by Little Wing
An imprint of Mango Books

18 Soho Square
London W1D 3QL
www.LittleWingBooks.com

HOW
TO BE A
ROCK
STAR

'LOSE YOUR DREAMS
AND YOU MIGHT LOSE YOUR MIND.'

MICK JAGGER

IN MEMORIAM PETER GREEN

29 October 1946 – 25 July 2020

Peter was a special person. A lyricist, a guitarist, a songwriter, an arranger, a poet. Of all the guitarists I have ever known, he was the only intellectual among them, and a truly unique talent. I doubt we'll ever see his like again.

To Angie, Barney, Katie and Rory.
Everything I do.

★

FOR TERRY WESTON

Terry and I met by chance through our mutual passion for and love of music. He owned a staggering collection of electric guitars, some of which I had the joy of playing. As he and I got to know each other, Terry became enthralled by my story. He set about trying to help me 'get it out there'. This process took much longer than either of us could have imagined. It is entirely due to his belief, tenacity and generosity that we succeeded. Thank you, Terry, for everything.

CONTENTS

FOREWORD

BY MICK FLEETWOOD

What a pleasure to be sitting in, writing about my lifelong friend Dave Ambrose! …and yes, 'lifelong' is a phrase not lightly-used…

In those early years, not long after we met, we were driven by the music that brought us together. It all started with our rhythm-section work in the band the Peter B's, which morphed into Shotgun Express with Rod Stewart and Beryl Marsden on vocals. Those were groundbreaking bands for me as a drummer. In truth, many lessons were learned playing alongside Dave which would stand me in good stead for all my playing years ahead. One of the most important lessons that I learned from him was, and still is, that "it has to swing," no matter what!

Reflecting back on those early bands, you can see trace elements of the embryonic beginnings of the core of Fleetwood Mac. That core was Peter Green, myself and Dave Ambrose.

Dave was asked to be the bass player in Fleetwood Mac. Hold that thought. It was at that moment in time that he made a decision to seek out other musical opportunities. But I'll leave that for him to recount! However, one thing was for sure: it was a decision that would lead him to many different creative endeavours in the music world. Later on, he would start working in the record industry. Due to his passion as a player, he rapidly excelled. His incredible music knowledge and understanding of musicians helped him to sign some major acts and to nurture the very best talent. While working as the director of A&R at EMI, he also looked after the likes of Queen and Pink Floyd. This truly shows the groundbreaking vision he had for music.

Although the drummer and the bass player took different paths, we each found our way in this crazy industry. We were both blessed with great success, which I for one attribute without question to those early, formative years.

Dave, congratulations on your beautiful book. A heartfelt thanks from me for your unconditional friendship and support. My God, how amazing it is to know that this story is "not over."

With love,
Mick Fleetwood

INHALE...

I have a dream, most nights, about hanging with a fantasy supergroup. The line-up rarely changes. On the kit, the coolest drummer, Charlie Watts. Silent, solid, sardonic Charlie, seeing all, saying little. What a player. In all senses. He listens to the notes. He gives a guitarist room. He's what they call a musician's musician. The rock star lifestyle never went to his head. Can you believe that he still takes the bus? Whenever a fellow passenger says to him, as one does every now and then, 'You look like that bloke out of the Rolling Stones,' he responds, 'So they tell me. Wouldn't it be nice.'

If Charlie's busy that night, I might call Phil Collins. Then again, he can be a dick. He's not someone I really want to hang with. Second thoughts, forget Phil and get me Aynsley Dunbar. I love the old Scouser. He might be the greatest in the world. That's him on Bowie's *Aladdin Sane*, *Pin-Ups* and *Diamond Dogs*. He drummed for Lennon and Lou Reed, Zappa, Hendrix, Ian Hunter, Jefferson Starship, and for my favourite lead guitarist, Jeff Beck: the maniac, the improvisor, the wild, daring, imaginative technician of whom I can never get enough. I salivate at the thought of Beck. Did I say 'favourite'? Better qualify: I hate the bastard. He fired me because bloody Ronnie Wood, who was supposed to be my mate, demanded to play guitar with him in my place. So Ronnie owes me.

My rhythm guitarist is fiercely wistful Johnny Marr, a miraculous man of incomparable magnetism. On keys, Duran Duran's Nick Rhodes. One, because he's sensational. Two, because I can never tell what he's thinking, and I always want to know. If he's too busy, it'll be Queen's old faithful Spike Edney, a plodder with flair. On bass? You're looking at him, because we can no longer get the Ox. Immovable John

1

Entwistle, aka Thunderfingers, was the best in the world bar none.

My frontman is the one-man theatre known as Jagger. When all is said, done and eaten, a nice bunch of guys. Jagger over Plant? By Christ, any day. Mick has a searing sense of irony that goes right over most people's heads. I love that, it makes him very English. If you want to know why he's survived for so long, there's your answer. He's a parody of himself. He can stomach the send-up. I remember him at a party once, sticking his arse in Simon Le Bon's face because Simon was trying to pull a model called Yasmin, and lustful Mick wanted her for himself. Simon married her in the end. They're still together thirty-odd years and however many kids later. So it's not true, whatever 'they' say. I've seen it with my own eyes. Not even the greatest showman can have it all.

★

Who in their right mind? You're asking me. I've been saying it for years and I'll say it again: you're off your head if you want to be a rock star. Easy life, you say? *What?* It'll render you bankrupt and drive you over the side sooner than make you rich and famous. How do I know? I was there. I climbed the charts, did the drugs, pulled the birds, strummed with the best of them: Mick Fleetwood, Rod Stewart, Ray Davies, Jeff Beck. I teetered on the brink of superstardom. I had it all, lost the lot, hit rock-bottom and almost succumbed to the inevitable, depression setting in and almost finishing me. I jacked it all in for steady jobs, only to be sucked right back into the music business for a second coming, discovering and breaking some of the most fantastic artists this country has ever produced: the Sex Pistols, Duran Duran, the Pet Shop Boys and more. I had a fine time making *them* rich and famous instead. I can tell you from bitter experience, it's a game that takes more than it gives. It sucks you dry and spits you out. It never makes a better person of anybody. It demands infinitely more than mere musical talent. You can be the most incredible prodigy – Elton John, say, who was teaching himself at the age of four, was having piano lessons at seven and won a scholarship to the Royal Academy of Music when he was eleven. Or Keith Emerson, who used to walk around with Beethoven sonatas under his arm, but could also play like Jerry Lee Lewis and Little Richard, so the school bullies left him alone. Or Rick Wakeman, taught formally from infancy, who played in school bands and progressed to the Royal College of Music before becoming a session guy for David Bowie, Cat Stevens and T. Rex. You've been playing better than them since you were in the womb, and you reckon it's your moment to make the leap? *Pause.*

The first thing you need to do if you're serious about being a rock star is to un-learn it all. Classical training is the most massive hindrance. It'll do you no favours. Punk was conjured by artists without musical talent who wanted to make music. Why not? It was different, and rock'n'roll is nothing if not about being different. The conundrum caught on. It gelled and it swelled. Punk proved that what you need above all else is attitude. You've got to have vision. You need to speak for the times you're living in, reflect what's going on down on the streets. You'd better do it with more pluck, spunk, style, élan and perseverance than the countless thousands of other wannabes. You have then got to grow a hide thicker than a pachyderm's, because you are going to get beaten.

You've got to be cool. It's essential that you are. Most musicians are. They have to be, in order to survive. You can't learn to be cool, you either are or you're not, which is the problem. You have to know your market, and be au fait with the latest trends. Fashion and trends are crucial. You need to know your licks inside-out, and keep updating them. The drummer who plays old-fashioned licks soon dates. His 'phone stops ringing. The same goes for guitarists, vocalists, keyboardists, brass. You've got to be a sharp businessman. Most successful rock musos are terrific hustlers. You're going to trust someone else to do it for you? A manager, you say? Good luck with that.

People often ask me who I admire and respect most in this game. I have a few up my sleeve, but today, I give you Madonna. The ability to reinvent yourself over and over is gigantic, but you still have to work at it as though your life depends on it. It takes nerve. Stamina. Phenomenal energy. Madge has all that. She works round the clock; she'll sleep when she's dead. Bowie was doing it before her, to music that was always thrilling and tasteful. Lady Gaga has done it since, look at her go. Don't be alarmed, either, by the extent to which so many modern musicians seem to rip each other off. Plagiarism is par for the course. It's nothing new. The classical musicians were all at it in the old days. There were no lawyers back then, which is the rub. The legal profession runs the music industry today. Don't allow anyone to convince you otherwise.

It's vital that you write your own songs. It's what gives you identity. It's the skill that lends meaning to everything else you do. It's the point of doing it. A rock'n'roll poet like Bob Dylan is really no different from the guy in tights with a lute, wandering from village to hamlet in days of old, centuries before newspapers. The task of the minstrel is to think hard about the message, to couch it in compelling and memorable terms, to deliver it artfully, and to keep coming back with more and more ideas. You think that's easy? Show me yours.

Then there's the dark side. That old back-biting, back-stabbing, back-beating dark side. Where shall we start? You want betrayal, isolation, exploitation, emotional upheaval, psychological damage, booze, drugs, women, men, sex? You have come to the right place. Take sex: bombarded from every angle, in every variation and combination, obsessing and possessing even those who might think they are immune. Rock'n'roll and sex are indivisible. Always have been. I wish I didn't have to say that I found girls back in the day so appallingly badly-behaved. I spent more time chucking chicks out of my bed than eating dinner. I have tried down the years to analyse it, and I can only blame my instrument. The guitar is the ultimate phallic symbol. Those masturbatory moves, all that strumming and plucking, drive women wild. I can remember when a good night was five hundred down and a fleet of ambulances. Kidding? What if I'm not? Be in no doubt: rock'n'roll is not only about the music. It is hardly at all about the music. Cast your mind back to Take That and Michael Jackson, grabbing their crotches and fiddling with their parts as if they were air guitars. It's irresistibly alluring, they tell me. Chuck in some suggestive lyrics. Think Lou Reed's 'Walk on the Wild Side': 'But she never lost her head, even when she was giving head.' The Beatles' 'Please Please Me,' which is about the same thing. 'I Touch Myself' by the Devinyls is obvious. Nick Jonas of the Jonas Brothers goes all-out and credits his sex life for his enlightened songwriting:

'Sexuality is important, as an artist, to embrace and use it as ammunition in your creative life, and understanding that part of your life and how it makes you feel,' he says. 'Anytime I approach writing a song, I think about the fact that since I started having sex, my creative life changed dramatically, as did my ability to write a song with more genuine depth, more reality.'

Ya think?

Too tame? How about Bowie banging Slash's mother Ola Hudson? The members of Mötley Crüe rubbing Mexican food into their genitals, 'dropping burritos in their laps' as they called it, to throw their girlfriends off the scent, which was eau de groupie? Sammy Hagar's legendary Van Halen sex tents? Queen's backstage cavortings with naked female mud wrestlers, and album launches featuring food served on the heads of bare-bottomed dwarfs? Super-groupie Cynthia Albritton, the infamous Plaster Caster, who spent the Seventies and Eighties making casts of musicians' penises? The Beach Boys, the Kinks and Jimi Hendrix all got nailed…

Above and beyond, you need something that sets you apart. But beware, your stand-out feature cannot be contrived. 'Dave, your accent's so fake, why do you put that on?' they used to taunt me, while the women drooled all over me. Fuck *them*. I talk posh because I went to a public school. Not my fault, is it? I didn't exactly have any say in the matter. I remember Jeff Beck once questioning my extensive nocturnal activity, because, in his words, 'But *Dave!* you seem like a real *gent!*' As if only sewer rats with elocution denser than phlegm were allowed to get laid. 'Let me tell you,' I responded, pointing with both hands at my flies, 'rock'n'roll is all down to one thing: *this.*' It's the reason why so many chancers who can't play competently, sing convincingly or write a half-decent song make it as artists. And you thought it was all about musical talent. Put the kettle on.

I am all too aware that we live in different, more enlightened times. Gross misconduct warnings are now written into record company contracts. The Musicians' Union publishes an email address via which individuals with concerns about sexism, harassment, sexual misconduct and actual assault can make themselves heard. Behaviour that might once have passed as 'just rock stars being rock stars' is no longer tolerated. Heritage rockers who once boasted about their conquests, long before the consent conversation kicked off, are now keeping schtum. Today's fans are more likely to regard the capers of the so-called good old days as disgraceful and indefensible. Where once they might have relished revelations of debauchery and have enjoyed the vicarious thrill, they now want something much more meaningful from their rock and pop idols. They want them to demonstrate awareness of eco- and socio-political issues. They want to be shown respect for their dedication, because after all it is the fans that keep a band alive. They want to see evidence of an attitude that condemns, rather than upholds and perpetuates, the feral larks of the rock'n'roll of old.

The groupie phenomenon that was once such a thing is much less of a thing now. Women have woken up to their worth. Most have more awareness and self-respect than to believe that there is value in surrendering themselves as the playthings of wild older men. The #MeToo movement has increased feminist activism and created a massive cultural shift. Change has happened rapidly. If you read Mötley Crüe's raw 2001 autobiography *The Dirt*, you probably turned a blind eye to Nikki Sixx's confession that he practically raped a drunken lass in a cupboard one night. The band's bassist and main songwriter then encouraged his drummer Tommy Lee to go in after him and do the same. Did the Crüe's fans fall away in droves? They did not. But if they were publishing such shocking revelations today, a couple of decades later, you can bet your life that their followers would have their guts for garters all over Twitter and Facebook, and that criminal proceedings might ensue – especially if the young lady in question summoned courage enough to bring legal proceedings. There have been cases of bands being dropped by their labels following allegations of sexual misconduct splashed all over social media. 'Consent' and 'male entitlement' are now the watchwords. Copious are the accounts of former groupies who have cause to question whether, as teenagers, they had any say in the matter, or whether in fact they were abused. Meeting the musicians you adore is one thing. Having sex with them is obviously another. It is difficult for most people to accept that there are factions of fans who actively seek sex with their favourite rock stars for the sexual act's own sake, if only for the bragging rights. Reader, it happens. It *still* happens. I think back to Pamela Des Barres, an infamous groupie who bedded Jimmy Page, Jim Morrison, Mick Jagger and many others, and who penned half a dozen unapologetic books about her exploits. She has always made clear that the sex was consensual, and explained her motivation as being her way of 'getting close to the music' in a compelling and feminist way. It's another side of the argument, with which most will doubtless not agree. But we cannot deny that some modern women are attuned to their sexuality, are turned on by rock stars, and enjoy the experience of mutual sexual experiences with musicians. Can it ever be equal? When one is rich and famous and the other is not? I'd have to say not. There is definitely a sense in today's music industry that groupie-ism is one of the last taboos. That the groupies themselves, if they are still going for it, are supposed to keep their mouths shut. 'Wham bam thank-you Ma'am' remains the unspoken rule. Lori Mattix has spoken about losing her virginity to David Bowie at the age of fourteen, following which she had an affair with Jimmy Page. She said that she never thought of herself as a groupie, but that she now wonders, with hindsight, whether what they did with her was wrong.

'I don't think underage girls should sleep with guys,' the now sixty-something admits. 'I wouldn't want this for anybody's daughter. My perspective is changing as I get older and more cynical.'

★

Despite my privileged education, I never got into classical music. It wasn't my thing. I discovered Elvis Presley, Eddie Cochran and the Everlys at the age of eleven, and that was me, done-for. I was soon playing standards at strip clubs while women peeled off their clothes. My eyes, which at first were everywhere, trying not to look and trying desperately to look, were opened early. Tony Secunda, a flamboyant pop manager who looked after the Move, the Moody Blues, Procol Harum, T. Rex and others, offered me a £25,000 contract at seventeen to become a rock star on his roster. I had the contract in my hand. I thought I was hearing and seeing things. I assumed he must be having me on, or that he had mistaken me for someone else. Because I couldn't play for a free bun. I couldn't sing a note. I certainly couldn't write anything. Not yet. But I had *hunger*. That, and a burning need to *do* something, to *be* somebody, which he must have detected a mile off. It's what it takes.

Tony had that acute sense of smell unique among the best rock managers. Simon Napier-Bell had it, and was hugely successful with the Yardbirds, Marc Bolan and Wham! Bennett Glotzer practically hallucinated odours. The relentless Sixties New York lawyer who represented songwriters, managed Frank Zappa and Blood, Sweat and Tears and who, in partnership with Bob Dylan's manager Albert Grossman, handled the careers of the Band, Janis Joplin, Gordon Lightfoot, Tom Rush and Paul Butterfield, had a brazen disdain for anyone who was not him. He always addressed a room with 'Hi, cuntsuckers.' 'Colonel' Tom Parker steered and ripped off Elvis. Tony Defries did much the same for Bowie. Ruthless south Londoner Peter Grant – gigantic, persuasive, a former film extra and bouncer at the Soho 2i's coffee bar, who became, some say, the greatest rock manager ever – had it with knobs. It scored him Led Zeppelin, for whom he emphasised albums over singles and live performances over television appearances, taking their net worth stratospheric and creating an entirely new blueprint for artist management.

Pete Waterman had it too, on a lesser scale. The PWL producer and songwriter created a white poor man's Tamla Motown that was so successful, I offered him a million quid to bring it to EMI when I was Head of A&R there. Why? Because he had an uncanny ability not only to identify and pick hits, but to select the appropriate artists to sing them: Kylie Minogue, Rick Astley, Dead or Alive, Bananarama, Mel and Kim, Jason Donovan. Most of them were not exceptional singers. Only Kylie can be said to have enjoyed real longevity. It was all quite predictable hi-NRG stuff, but it hit the spot at a moment in time. His acts *had something*. Of which Waterman was well aware. He didn't need us. He turned us down.

Which brings me to The One Thing. The so-called Unique Selling Point. The quality that makes an artist different from everyone else. What else could it be but their own dysfunctional childhood, the ways in which they were forced or just happened to evolve? Drawing on the pain and challenges of their miserable little backgrounds, the best of them manage to come up with and lend shape to music that resonates with millions. It takes a rare creative muscle to be able do something so extraordinary. Few are born with it. Those who are can't fathom it. Seriously, they have absolutely no idea where it comes from. Neither do I. All I know, all *anybody* knows, is that if you are blessed with it, you have to keep using it. Take it for granted and it soon turns to flab…

ORIGINS

Rock'n'roll is about validation. It's about a burning need to be someone… or to be someone other than who you really are. Such need is usually born of neglect, abuse and abandonment. I was a victim of all three from a very young age. Privileged white kid? Awash with dosh? Expensive education? How bad can it have been? As dysfunctional as it comes, if you want to know. Nothing is ever as it seems.

I was born Edmund David Ambrose on 11th December 1945, less than three months after the end of World War II. I have never until now really given much thought to how that was for my mother Andrée, a young, displaced Frenchwoman who was pregnant during wartime, giving birth in a foreign country, not knowing what kind of world she was bringing a child into, nor whether she would ever see home and family again. Mum was an impoverished Baptist minister's daughter from Brittany who had been sent to England to escape Nazi occupation while her brothers Jean and Daniel fought in the French Resistance, supported by the rest of the clan. My father Jack, known as Professor E. J. Ambrose, was the son of a wealthy and benevolent master builder. He was also a gifted graduate of Emmanuel College, Cambridge, with a Double First Class Honours degree in Physics and Biology and a calling to become a research scientist. While staying with family friends Mimi and Bill in Cambridge, Mum met her future husband on a kind of blind date. As family folklore has it, she first set eyes on him skating in the Fens, and was felled by his athleticism and grace. Opposites attracted: he the outgoing, sporty academic, she the demure, elusive 'musical one', who would accompany herself on the harmonium as she sang hymns she had learned as a child. Both my parents were deeply religious, which was possibly the X-factor, the common denominator via which they bonded. Dad had been motherless since the age of twelve, when my grandmother died of cancer. Bereaved children often marry young and start families of their own quite quickly, as if to compensate for the elements missing from their childhood. Dad was no exception. They wasted no time in having me. My sister Philippa followed three years later, on 27th July 1948. Her arrival didn't impress me much, but that soon changed. I lived in my own fantasy world. The moment she was old enough, she quickly became part of it. To me, she was enchanting. A beautiful little girl.

Our family moved from London's Highgate Village to Maidenhead, twenty-five miles west of the capital.

It was of no concern to me as a child, but it upsets me to think of it now. Each successive move conveyed my mother further from France. Now that she was married, with children of her own, it was obvious that she was never going back to Brittany. Although she did not complain, not to me, at least, the realisation must have devastated her. It went over my head as a child. But when I think of her now, in the final third of my own life, I see in my mind's eye a rather sad, troubled woman consumed by silent desolation. Despite the fact that she had married a well-to-do Englishman and lived the life of the affluent wife, she never became 'British'. There was always something dislocated about her, as though she were here under sufferance, only temporarily, and that she secretly longed to go home. It's possible that I sensed that as a child, and that it frightened the life out of me. The thought of her ever leaving me, of never seeing her again, was the most terrifying thing of all. While she adored her children and my father, there was something about her that made her seem 'not one of us.' Of course she missed her parents, her siblings, the fairytale house she had grown up in, which had its own well; the wild Breton coast, the sea, the cuisine, her native language. She loved us to bits, as much as any mother could. I know now that she was consumed by a longing that would never heal. The thought of it breaks my heart.

I was a most peculiar little boy. A loner from an early age. I think I knew that about myself at the time, but I can't say that it bothered me.

I inhabited a world of make-believe entirely of my own creation. I am aware that it is common for children to conjure imaginary friends, which usually take the form of angels or other children: an exotic cousin, say, or the big brother you wished you had. My own, however, were of the animal kingdom. I befriended all kinds of creatures. I would round them up each day and make sure they went with me when I was whipped off to nursery school. When I contracted measles at the age of seven and fell very ill with double pneumonia, I was placed in confinement quite far from home, in London's St. George's Hospital. My extended isolation brought my animal pals into their own, for a while at least. But I soon grew bored, frustrated and disruptive in hospital. When at last I was deemed well enough to go home, I'm sure the doctors, nurses and other staff there were very glad indeed to see the back of me.

While Maidenhead was sufficiently distant from London not to be paralysed by London's killer fogs during the early Fifties, I was in desperate need of cleaner air than I was able to breathe at home. A move to the country was deemed desirable, indeed necessary. More than forty miles south-east the family now headed, to a beautiful area of England known as the North Downs. Home would henceforth be Hartswood Manor, a small estate with stables which Dad would convert into our new home. Not strictly-speaking 'countryside', being within easy reach of Reigate, we were at least surrounded by farms and forest that made it seem much more remote than it was. We had access to our own bluebell wood, where Philippa and I would rollick for hours on end, and where I could freely breathe the sweetest, freshest air. I soon got better.

All kids hark back to a period of their childhood which they consider to have been their happiest. I think both Philippa and I knew, even as we were living it, that those heavenly Hartswood Manor days would be the best of our lives. There are times when I can hardly bear to think of those days, so perfectly are they preserved in my memory. For a start, it was always summer. We'd be out of doors from breakfast until supper. We lived next to a farm, and Philly struck up a loyal friendship with Ena, the farmer's daughter. She helped with the cows, and fell in love with two carthorses called Ginger and Jolly. We helped plough the fields, round up the sheep and milk the cows. There were no milking machines in those days as the farm did not yet have electricity, so they still had bonnet-wearing milkmaids. One day we found the wreckage of a World War II biplane which had crashed into the River Mole. We were terrified, fearful that we would find the skeleton of the pilot still inside. Our fears were soon allayed. We turned the plane into a raft and played pirates on it. We spent so much time on the farm, sleeves up, knees bare, charging about to our hearts' content. We went fishing, gathered berries from hedgerows, and larked about with the sun on our faces until the cows came home. We took things apart and put them back together again. We made do and mended. I became an enthusiastic drawer and painter of pictures of whatever I could find and see, and developed a love of art that would last me my lifetime. If I could have given my own children any choice of childhood, anywhere at all, I would have given them exactly what my sister and I had. The summers die, one by one. How soon they fly...

Burys Court was my independent prep school in Reigate. It was, strictly speaking, a boarding school. There was no need for me to board, however, as we lived close enough for me to go home every afternoon. I was enrolled as a day boy and rode my bike there each day, resentful at having to leave my little sister behind. I think I knew, young as I was, almost from the first week of my first term there, that I was never going to make a scholar. That I would never follow in my father's footsteps, reach his hallowed alma mater, or distinguish myself in any academic way. I would sit by the window and day-dream, watching the world go by, and imagining myself anywhere but at my desk, chanting times tables. I was bored senseless by the work, most of which went in one ear and straight out the other. My disruptive nature got the better of me, and I was always being summoned to see the Head. My most sinister memory of my time at Burys Court is of the Latin master, who abused me. We didn't know in those days that we could object to a teacher running his hands up your thighs while he chastised you. Perhaps I did know that it was wrong, but I never told anyone. Something stopped me. Maybe I thought I wouldn't be believed, or that I might be blamed for it in some way. That I'd get into much more trouble than I was already in. So I would put such horrible incidents to the back of my mind, and leave those unclean, uncomfortable memories behind as I raced home on my bike to get back to my sister, my mother, my wonderful home, and to my painting. I adored my family, and they adored me. I loved my life, and I never wanted it to change. I could not envisage a time when it ever would.

But then it did. I was ten years old, and I remember it clearly. Without a by your leave, a kiss goodbye or even a forwarding address, my mother and father left us.

2
FORSAKEN

I knew there was something wrong the moment I ran into the house. Mum wasn't there. My godmother Aunt Mimi was there in her place, being all breezy and busy and smiling too much. Philippa was sitting on the sofa by herself, her face in her hands, staring into space. She didn't even look up when I came in. 'Where's Mum?' I asked her. She didn't say a word. Out in the kitchen, Aunt Mimi poured me a glass of milk and sat me down at the table. 'Your mother and father have had to go away for a while,' she said.

'Why?' was all I could think of to say. '*Why*?' I whined the word over and over, but it didn't get me anywhere. What had happened to them? Why hadn't they told us they were going? 'You'll have such fun on the farm,' said Aunt Mimi firmly, every time I asked her, to the point that I thought I must be going mad. I wanted to scream. Why did they just leave without saying goodbye? Why didn't they wait for me to come home from school? Why couldn't they have come to my school to tell me themselves? Why, why, *why*? No matter how many times Mimi reassured us that everything was going to be all right, that they'd soon be back, I had a terrible sense of foreboding. My worst nightmare had come true. Mum must have run off back to France at long last, unable to bear the separation from her 'real' family any longer. Dad must have gone after her, where he would be on his knees, begging and pleading with her to return, and she would be having none of it, and I was never going to see my darling mother again. I couldn't bear it. I must have made this happen myself, by thinking such a terrible thing in the first place. I wanted to be sick. I felt frozen inside my head and my heart, an awful intense chilliness, like I'd been stabbed with picks of ice. You hear the phrase 'my blood ran cold' and wonder what that feels like. I knew exactly what that felt like, that day. My temples pulsated. My veins were dark blue. I wanted to fall on the floor and die. I looked at Philippa and she looked at me. Neither of us spoke. We had always been close, but now we clung to each other. We were all that we had. Aunt Mimi's no-nonsense kindness was all very well. It did nothing to dispel the fear that our parents were never coming back, and that my sister and I were now truly alone.

It got worse. The dominoes fell one by one, each toppled by the last, until life as we knew it had collapsed.

Philly and I were moved on, to stay with friends of my parents for several months. Then my godmother Mimi stepped in again, and took me to stay with them at Wadhurst Park, near the Kent/East Sussex border, another hour beyond Tunbridge Wells. We didn't take Philly, and I didn't know why. I was desperately worried about her. She was only seven years old, and I had no idea where she was. Adults were not very good at explaining things to children in those days. We simply did as we were told, and didn't ask questions. Where were Mum and Dad now? When were they coming back? Would they *ever* be coming back? I could only wonder.

After a year or so, Philly did come to stay with us. We attended the local school, where poor little Philly did nothing but cry all the time. We were told this new arrangement was 'only for the time being,' and that things would soon be back to normal. Even though I was no great fan of school, I began to fear that I would never see Burys Court again. I was too young at the time to articulate my thoughts concisely, but I know now that my sense of security was threatened. Philippa's too. A child needs to know where he belongs, and to whom. He needs familiarity and routine. He needs not only to be fed and watered, he depends on daily affection and reassurance. Only when these things are withdrawn do we realise how greatly we rely on them.

I worried about everything. About our home, Hartswood Manor, and what would become of it. Who would look after the place? Would somebody else have moved in? Would they be wearing our clothes, playing with our toys, lounging around on our furniture, using our plates and cutlery, cooking with our pots and pans? I pictured strangers lying in my bathtub, brushing their teeth at my basin, gathering flowers and berries from my hedgerows. I overthought absolutely everything, and started driving myself mad. I feared every worst thought about my parents. Mum must have been captured by military forces, she must have been taken against her will. Dad's boat had surely been caught in a swell during a stormy crossing to Brittany, and he had obviously been drowned at sea. I went to bed each night, but I barely slept. We don't really toss and turn, do we. We lie still, as stiff as corpses, listening out for every little thing, a key in the door, the hoot of an owl, a raised voice, a cry; some sign that all of this had been a nightmare, and that I would soon wake up again to normal life. To begin with, I counted the weeks since Mum and Dad had vanished. As the seasons consumed the months, I didn't dare do that anymore. I grew afraid of Christmas, of New Year, of Easter, of long school summer holidays, of my birthday, of all the celebrations that remind you that another year has passed. I felt like a prisoner, trapped in my over-active imagination, all the while trying to reassure Philippa that everything was going to be all right. Convinced, in my heart, that it couldn't be. I tried so hard to remember everything about Mum and Dad, the colour of their eyes, the shape of their noses, the little wrinkles and bumps, their hands, their fingers. The feel of my mother's soft hand when she smoothed my face if I'd been crying. The weight of my father's arms as he hugged me gently to him. Nothing. The harder I reached for them, the more surely the memories faded. I wanted to draw and paint them, to capture the memory of them, but I didn't dare. I knew in my heart that I would never see them again.

But then I did. Mimi announced one day that Mum had come back. We rushed to see her. I remember her lying on a bed, staring back at us but not speaking. We were speechless too. After a while, Dad followed her home. Nobody said anything. How is a child supposed to process that? It was cruel.

My parents looked different, yet exactly the same. I knew that I must seem changed to them after such a long absence, Philippa too, though neither of them remarked on it. I stared at them and saw my beloved mother and father, just as they had always been. I also saw two complete strangers. I searched their faces for answers, in vain. I adored them, and was so happy to see them, but I also felt angry; so angry at times that I thought I might explode. How could they have done this to us? Did they have any idea of the damage they had caused? Why couldn't they have told us that they were going away, or have reassured us that they would definitely be coming back? Why had they left us dangling in agony for so long? It does seem curious to me now that they never explained it. I couldn't ask them. I was only a child.

I have a few vague memories now of Philippa and me getting ready to return home. Grabbing all our things together, uniform and sports kit and sponge bags and weekend clothes, books and homework and toys, my paints, pencils and brushes, shoes, boots, plimsolls. I can see us loading up the car and all climbing in together, and embarking on the not-very-long drive that seemed to take forever. Could we really be going back to Hartswood Manor, or were they now about to drop us somewhere else, and abandon us again? Had they only looked in to make sure that we were doing okay without them? The concept of 'going home' seemed too good to be true. I hardly dared to imagine that it was really happening. Not until we turned into the drive and approached the old house that Dad had made for us out of stables could I begin to believe that the nightmare was finally over. Not that it was. Because my innocence had been stolen from me. The childish exuberance to which every infant has a right had drained out of me, never to return. I found that I could no longer take anything for granted. They had done this to us once. What was to stop them going off again? How could we trust them? Never again would I climb the stairs to bed in the certain knowledge that my mother and father would be there to greet me with a hug and a kiss in the morning.

★

When I returned to my old school in Leigh, I had been gone for two academic years, but still managed to get my Common Entrance. I was now twelve years old, and Philly was ten. She went to a little school in Reigate, where she was happy. She moved on to Reigate County School for Girls, where she excelled. She was a brilliant swimmer, particularly at breaststroke, and was always winning cups in competitions.

Many years would pass before I found out the truth. My father had suffered a total psychological breakdown in Paris, and had been admitted to a psychiatric hospital there. He had become incapable of functioning in everyday life, and unable to face ordinary challenges and daily routine. Terrifying and isolating for him, this must also have been bewildering and shocking for my poor mother. She must have felt, not that it was ever explained, that his need of love and support was greater than that of her children. Perhaps she decided that we would cope better if we were left in the dark, and spared the gory details. Perhaps she simply didn't have the words or sufficient understanding herself to be able to share the situation with Philippa and me in ways that we could comprehend. It's also likely that she was afraid of what the truth might do to us. Either way, it was never discussed. They were back. It was for us to fear, as we did for the remainder of our childhood, that they might easily disappear again. I never again felt as close to them as I had before they left us. I had learned, to a certain extent, to stand on my own two feet. That was the impression I gave, at least. I had become a coper. I never shared with another soul the insecurity and sadness that were eating away at me inside. I probably needed therapy. Years of it. That kind of thing wasn't the norm back then. Too late now.

Although I now regarded my father rather differently, and could no longer trust him, he remained the object of my adoration for a very long time. Not that, I must now admit, I knew very much about him.

Who was he? A professor named Jack. He had a significant job of some sort, though he never really talked about it. I had gleaned that he was involved in scientific work at London's Institute of Cancer Research, and that he was also something to do with radar operations over in Teddington. He was rather secretive about the ways in which he earned the money on which we lived. In those post-war years, there was a lot of that about. Secrecy. People must have felt that they were not yet out of the woods. The threat of annihilation, of the world being wiped out, loomed large during the 1950s. I knew that Dad was a scientist, and I think I fantasised that he was some kind of spy. I imagined him immersed in all kinds of thrilling, dare-devil scenarios. He had an impenetrable air about him, as well as a quiet charm. I felt drawn to him. I wanted to be like him. I was never going to be. The aspect of him that I resisted was his tendency towards black moods. I didn't know about mood swings back then. I know now that he had an ongoing susceptibility towards depression. The look of him during his frequent attacks was a terrifying thing. He didn't look like himself. He would take himself off to a deckchair in the garden and would sit there, staring, at nothing in particular. I would have no idea what to say or do to make him feel better. My mother would notice me watching him. She was very caring and concerned, and she would do her best to comfort him. Once or twice, she made odd in-passing remarks about his condition being related to 'what the Russians did to him.' I didn't have a clue what she was on about. Nor did I ever find out.

★

They sent me back to Burys Court. I should have been happy about that, but my heart wasn't in it. If I was never going to make an academic before the trauma of my parents' disappearance, I was bound to be a miserable failure now. I became even more beholden to my daydreams. I dropped to the bottom of the class in pretty well every subject. Except art. I was beginning to show a real grasp of form and perspective and was developing an individual style, though the latter was sinister. I had started to paint my mind. My pictures were inhabited by phantom-like creatures reminiscent of Edvard Munch's 'The Scream'. His disturbing work is said to have been inspired by anxiety, real or imagined. The tormented individuals in my own paintings were manifestations of the torture I was suffering in my head. I realise that this might sound far-fetched in such a young child, but I know that it was real. Although I think they were careful to try and disguise it, I clocked the worried looks on the faces of my teachers. I don't know whether they ever discussed with my parents the feelings I must have been trying to express through my pictures. If they did, it never filtered down to me.

★

I'd never heard of Elvis Presley when I first heard 'Heartbreak Hotel'. I've listened to plenty of people talking since about the moment he crashed their lives, about the song that changed their world forever. It was released in the UK in May 1956, and by June had got to Number Two in the charts. It would linger there for several months more.

John Lennon said it came to him via Radio Luxembourg when he was sixteen years old:

'...I could hardly make out what was being said. It was just the

19

experience of hearing it and having my hair stand on end. We'd never heard American voices like that …suddenly there's this hillbilly hiccupping on tape echo and all the blues stuff going on …to us, it just sounded as a noise that was great.'

George Harrison, three years younger, reckoned it was his 'rock'n'roll epiphany'. Keith Richards, then twelve, said it was the first rock'n'roll he ever heard, and that he was amazed by it. Robert Plant, eight at the time, would claim that the song changed his life, being 'the first musical arousal I ever had.'

It changed my life too. Boy, did it change it. I was a most impressionable eleven-year-old. Sitting there at home poring over my Greek homework with Radio Luxembourg on in the background, the song came on, this incredible gurgle of a voice, this throbbing insistent sound. The lyrics were a jumble, but I caught phrases like 'Lonely Street' and 'I get so lonely I could die,' and I thought, 'Who is this? This chap is singing about *me*!' I knew nothing about the song, the events that might have inspired the writing of it, the singer, the musicians, where it was recorded, the label it was released on. I knew barely anything about the United States of America itself at that point, let alone the amazing new rock stars emerging during the Fifties. All I knew was what I was hearing there and then, in the moment. Everything about it thrilled me to bits. It struck me as the delivery of a promise, the shape of things to come. I heeded the clarion call. Who the hell was Elvis Presley? At that point, I could hardly have cared less. What mattered was that he knew who *I* was.

3

AWAKENING

What a revelation. One minute the only music in my life was birdsong in the hedgerows, the reassuring drone of hymns, the odd bit of classical, the stuff we were force-fed at school. The next, an entire universe of completely new sounds opened up to me, and my ears sprang to life. I could access this new music free on the radio or for the price of a record from a music shop in Reigate. It was miraculous. It changed my life. It might even have saved it.

I had no inkling at that point about the rich, eclectic history of American music, born of diverse cultures carried all the way from far-flung corners to a single, gigantic country; of the ways in which boogie-woogie, rockabilly, R&B, swing-band, Dixieland jazz and honkytonk country and western – ghetto music, hillbilly music – were converging. I knew nothing of cross-pollination or mutual influence, nor even what those phrases meant. I was as yet unaware of the significance of places like Chicago, Memphis, New Orleans or New York, places I never imagined for the life of me that I'd get to see. Though I would soon know the names of the trailblazers – Fats Waller, Cab Calloway, Howling Wolf, B.B. King, Johnny Cash, Jerry Lee Lewis, Carl Perkins, Ike Turner, Fats Domino, Little Richard, Elvis himself – I was a million miles from understanding the first generation of rock'n'roll. I had no idea that the term itself was black slang for having sex. When I found that out later, it made sense. All I knew was that I liked it, and that I wanted more. It would all too soon occur to me that sex and music have more than a little in common.

More than anything, what this new music represented to me was freedom. It gave me a life that was nothing to do with my parents. Much of it sounded downright dangerous. I knew it was probably something they wouldn't like. It helped me to detach myself and become more independent of them. It energised and inspired me, and projected me into a mysterious place that only the like-minded could access. It would soon transform me, helping me to express aspects of my deeply complex personality hitherto suppressed. It would seduce me completely. It would keep me listening and playing for life. There and then, it excited me in ways I didn't yet understand.

There would come the time when I would find myself reflecting on Plato, the ancient Greek philosopher, and a declaration, made in his *The Republic* in about 375 BC. Among his many observations came the warning that significant changes in types of music lead unavoidably to sweeping changes in society overall. He saw this as a bad thing, and recommended that the government seize control of musical expression and the styles in which it was performed, in order to contain potential unruliness and maintain control. A similar thing came to pass during the 1950s, when the music of the black man began to seep into the ears of the white kids, and terrified parents, teachers and politicians scrabbled to stamp the inclination out. They failed miserably, for a simple reason. Until then, there had been music for adults, and there had been music for children. Nothing in between. Those in transition from childhood to adulthood were going through cataclysmic changes, but had no music of their own through which to express and process that. Suddenly, they did. It was long-overdue. There was such desire and need for it that rock'n'roll was always going to mushroom out of control. Hence, teenagers: the new, all-American invention foisted upon the world, giving the youth of the world their voice. I was not yet a teenager myself, at that stage, but I wasn't far off. Elvis, Eddie Cochran, the Everly Brothers: all the Es. I lapped them up, and was desperate to be just like them.

While the UK produced its own steady stream of popular recording artists, to my mind it couldn't hold a candle to what was coming out of America. If those so-called heart-throb artists seemed manufactured, they were: by cigar-chomping, suit-wearing, flash-car-driving 'managers' who trawled the nation for baby-faced boys, restyling, renaming and launching them on an unsuspecting public, who would fall in love with them and hang on their every crooned syllable. In some ways an inspired move, the discerning music-lover (as I was already kidding myself I'd become) could only regard such practice as cynical. With a superiority born mainly of ignorance, I rejected that initial wave of British pop artists and saved my pocket money for the real thing flooding in from over the pond. But the Brits were definitely getting better at it. I surrendered to the obvious talent of Marty Wilde and Billy Fury. I was moved by 'Move It', which as it turned out was written by Ian 'Sammy' Samwell for Harry Webb, whom he'd met in The 2i's Coffee Bar in Soho in 1958. Harry metamorphosed into Cliff Richard and had a hit with that great song, with his band the Drifters, of which Samwell became one. The Marquee Club opened on Oxford Street that year, where the Rolling Stones would perform their first gig in 1962. Brian Jones, Eric Clapton and a host of other young musicians moved in on Soho, and took up residence. It was fast becoming the place to be. I wasn't yet aware of Stock Records on South Molton Street on the other side of Regent Street, who had all the imports: blues, R&B, rock'n'roll. Chuck Berry, Little Milton, Bo Diddley, 'Queen of the Blues' Koko Taylor. But it wouldn't be long.

Then suddenly came skiffle. The revival of an earlier craze in America, it was a blend of folk, blues and jazz that was played on home-made instruments, and which is now considered to have been the precursor of punk. This was music that absolutely anybody could make, with a tea-chest, broom-handle, bits-of-string bass and your mother's old laundry washboard on which to scrape a rhythm. It echoed the sleeves-up, make-do-and-mend mentality of how we British coped during the war years, and it captured the national imagination. 'Rock Island Line', the cover by Lonnie Donegan played on Radio Luxembourg, ignited everyone's imagination. If you're old enough, you may remember it:

'The Rock Island Line is a mighty good road
The Rock Island Line is the road to ride...'

An old American folk song from the 1920s, it had been recorded by all kinds, from prisoners to railroad workers to Lead Belly: an American folk and blues singer-songwriter otherwise known as Huddie William Ledbetter, who strummed a mean twelve-string guitar. Essentially an Arkansas Negro (as was the term in those days) convict song, it had now been purloined for the pleasure of the British listening audience. It not only became a massive hit here, but was sold back to America in classic coals-to-Newcastle style. Glaswegian-born Donegan went on to have thirty-one British Top 30 singles, twenty-four of them back-to-back and three of them Number Ones. He was also the first British artist to score two American Top 10 hits, and was our most successful and most influential artist ahead of the Beatles.

'Rock Island Line' was the penny-drop moment for so many musicians. Although it was recorded by many notable artists, George Melly, Bobby Darin, Johnny Cash and Woody Guthrie among them, and continues to be recorded in the 21st century by stars such as Ringo Starr and Billy Bragg, there is no beating dear old Donegan's 'original'. It was the first recording to achieve gold status in the UK, selling more than a million copies around the world. It also started a craze that became a national obsession. At one point, there were reckoned to be between thirty and fifty thousand skiffle groups all over the British Isles. Chas McDevitt's Skiffle Group, Johnny Duncan and the Bluegrass Boys, and the Vipers were among the most prolific. When the *Six-Five Special* produced by Jack Good launched on BBC television in 1957 – the first British youth music programme with a skiffle recording as its title track and featuring skiffle acts as well as pop artists the likes of Terry Dene, Petula Clark, Marty Wilde and Tommy Steele – seventeen-year-old John Lennon had already started to perform with his own Liverpool skiffle group, the Quarry Men. Their most notable appearances were in on the back of a truck in a field behind St. Peter's Church Woolton, and in the church hall opposite, on Saturday 6th July 1957 …the day that John first encountered a baby-faced fifteen-year-old by the name of James Paul McCartney.

My parents were delighted by my enthusiasm for music, my mother especially, being such a diligent musician herself. But no tea-chests, broom handles, bits of string or washboards for me. I was one of the privileged few whose family could afford proper lessons. My mother wanted Philippa and me to follow in her footsteps and play the piano. Dad decided it was only right that I should have a say in the matter. He invited a chap from the music shop to visit and chat to me about music, to help me decide which instrument I'd like to learn. He clearly had some experience of the sort of thing that inspired young folk, and came armed with a saxophone and a Spanish guitar. I couldn't take my eyes off the latter, it was love at first sight. Dad bought me the guitar and I began to practise immediately, while Philippa opted for piano lessons. You've heard that phrase 'He couldn't put it down'? That was me, night and day, driving my family nuts. The apathy with which I'd applied myself to my school lessons suggested an indifferent and listless boy who took advantages for granted and couldn't care less about getting good at anything, because 'family money' would always be there to cushion him. But the guitar changed all that. I was devoted to it, and determined to be as good as I could get. I practised chords over and over, until I was good enough to start copying the performances I heard on my favourite records. Buddy Holly's were the easiest, and I stuck with those for a bit. I studied musicians' fingers on the television music shows of the day, the afore-mentioned *Six-Five Special* and *Oh Boy!* as if my life depended on it. Maybe it did.

★

Despite a certain shyness and remoteness that I suspect were exacerbated by my parents' disappearance, and by an ongoing fear that it might happen again, there was always a performer in me. While I have long suffered to a certain extent from stage fright, Philippa and I had always loved to dress up and put on little plays for family and friends, usually pieces that we'd come up with ourselves and featuring characters from history, as well as ghosts. We were both fascinated by the paranormal, and would scare ourselves witless with the kind of stuff we conjured. It's fair to say that we both had incredibly vivid imaginations.

The leap from such elementary entertainment to feeling inclined to play my guitar for the enjoyment of other people was not too great. There was a boy at Burys Court with similar inclinations. It wasn't long before Clive Pickford and I were joined at the hip. I felt quite blessed that we found each other. At first we'd just hang around enthusing about Eddie Cochran and the rest. Before long, we were actually practising together. We soon got good enough to land ourselves a few casual gigs at Reigate's tennis club, where we'd play covers of our favourite hits at their regular dances. My sister would sometimes join in on piano, got up like Shirley Temple in the kind of sticky-out frocks that my mother adored her in, but which made Philippa squirm. Even at that young age, I realised that the stage was my natural habitat. That wasn't really me up there, thrashing out Eddie Cochran, Elvis Presley and Buddy Holly hits, but a variation of me, who came to life the moment we began to play. My alter ego was a bit of a cool dude, with a brooding gaze and a sardonic smile. He could narrow his eyes and blaze. He was a sexy little fuck, I like to think. He was getting there. Just before I left Burys Court for good, we had a gig at the school's Bean Feast. I remember one or two of the teachers staring at me in amazement, as if to say, 'What the... that *can't* be the Ambrose boy, he doesn't have it in him!'

★

I was certainly a fantasist, on a variety of levels. I loved the vast new subjects of Sci-Fi, the comics and the films, and the whole idea of space exploration too, which was then in its infancy. I was probably more than a bit obsessed with the ideas of 'the final frontier' and of alien invasion, as were many children of my age. We wouldn't have Doctor Who, the Time Lord from Gallifrey, or his space/time vehicle TARDIS until 1963. Commander Neil Armstrong would not become the first human to walk on the moon until six years after that. But I could wait. I hadn't at that point ingested any kind of forbidden substance, not even alcohol. Well, maybe a sneaky sip of beer here and there, or some stolen wine slurped from a parent's glass. I was as sure as I could be that I was in full possession of my faculties. It was with trepidation bordering on terror, therefore, that I stood in the shade of a tree in the fields beyond the back garden of Hartswood Manor with my father one afternoon, staring up at an enormous metallic-looking airborne object that could only be a UFO. I squinted, dazzled by sunlight. Was I seeing things? Could I be suffering from the same affliction that had caused Dad to take leave of his senses? Was whatever it was hereditary? My only hope of the assurance of ongoing sanity would be if he had seen it too. 'Do you see it, Dad, do you see it?' I cried, clutching at his arm.

'It's a flying saucer,' said Dad. What chilled me later, when I allowed myself to think about it, was that he didn't seem in the least surprised. This made me wonder even more about the kind of work that my father was involved in, the detail of which he never divulged. I am none the wiser to this day. I keep on wondering.

AWAKENING

★

Our idyllic, carefree summers at Hartswood Manor were drawing to a close. My childhood along with them. For reasons that were never explained to me – I was never any the wiser, children were the last to be consulted in those days – we packed up and left paradise for an imposing Victorian mansion in the middle of Reigate. Had my mother had her fill of the British countryside, and of relative isolation? This was never expressed, not within my earshot at least. Philippa knew less than I did. We had no choice but to go along with it. My father bought himself a rather posh car, a Bentley. He had news for me, too, and it wasn't good: I was about to be sent, whether I liked it or not, to boarding school.

4

BOARDER LINE

We tend to remember the things that happen around the time we start 'big' school. Perhaps even more so if our experience of secondary education takes place within the confines of a boarding school. Sounds idyllic, doesn't it... the privileged, fee-paying experience, in a majestic building in a beautiful location, with every imaginable facility and comfort. I can tell you first-hand, it is anything but. 'Boarding School Syndrome' may not yet have been identified during my own years of secondary education, but look at the damage it has done.

For the uninitiated, the syndrome applies to the millions of adults who suffer long-term emotional and/or behavioural difficulties as the result of having lost out on normal family life, because they were sent to live elsewhere to be educated. The psychological trauma of the privileged child is now 'a thing'. Children obviously change, constantly and rapidly. From one day to the next. When a child is brought up at home, his family evolves to accommodate his emotional and physical progress. Living together under the same roof allows parents to keep a close eye and to adapt and provide as necessary. But no educational institution can evolve around the needs of every individual child. What happens is that the child himself has to evolve and adapt to fit in with that establishment's regime. This shock to the system, together with the sudden and repeated loss of parents, siblings, toys, pets, the unique comforts of home, causes the child to shut down on his need for intimacy. He loses a fundamental part of himself that he might never regain. This can lead to catastrophe in adulthood: clinical depression; the inability to discuss or comprehend his emotions; a pre-determined need to escape from, or even destroy, his most meaningful relationships. Every divorcée once married to a former public-school boarder knows exactly what I'm talking about. They should console themselves with the fact that they probably never stood a chance, and that the collapse of their marriage was not their fault. It's a sad fact that most ex-public-school boarders do not make good spouses. Don't blame me, I didn't invent the tendency. I'm merely observing, and pointing out an uncomfortable truth. While it seems to be the case that such problems mostly afflict children forced to board from an early age, and that those sent away to school when they are older are less likely to suffer, it is a very real problem that was conveniently ignored for far too long. The fact that it is discussed openly now, and is recognised, has helped me enormously in my own recovery. I know now that I was not imagining things, and that I had a right to feel the way that I did. I identify with so much of what has been written on this subject, as if they are writing about me personally. I know others who feel the same. Sufferers do tend to hide their symptoms and give the stiff-upper-lip impression of capability and control. We tend to feel that we are not entitled to feel like victims of anything, because we had such a privileged start in life. We are sometimes in denial about our distress. I know I was, for a very long time. We are not the sort of people who find it easy to show our feelings, or to ask for help. We struggle with relationships of all kinds. We can be stunted emotionally. We swallow stress. We put on the brave face and sport it proudly, like a mask. We are icebergs of emotional stuntedness. We can't help it: we were raised in an era when it was normal to keep one's feelings to oneself.

Poor me, right? Come on, it's not all bad. What, other than all that misery, could have prepared me so perfectly for my life in rock'n'roll, which is nothing if not the mecca of dysfunctionality?

★

My father had intended for me to progress to Monkton Combe school at Combe Down, Bath, a hundred and twenty miles to the west. I was reluctant to be sent so far away from home, but I needn't have worried. I didn't have what it took to be accepted. Seaford College in Petworth, near Chichester, West Sussex agreed to take me in the end. This was at best third-best as far as my father was concerned, but would have to do. Perhaps the only good thing about it was that it was so much closer to home. Only about thirty miles away to be precise, and less than an hour's journey – to the point that I couldn't really see why I had to board at all. Couldn't I just travel to and from by train? Couldn't I be driven? I know people today whose children attend schools significantly further away from home than mine, but they are not made to board. Just saying. I could tell that my mother didn't want me to go at all, although the last thing she was going to do was protest to my dad. He, of course, was gung-ho about it, because boarding school was 'the done thing' for 'people like us'. He assured me that it would be a 'good, character-building experience'. I confess, I liked the look of the place when I first set eyes on it: a rather grand neo-classical edifice in Lavington Park, perched above the South Downs. I rather fancied myself as a master of all I surveyed in such an exquisite setting. Its outward appearance betrayed nothing of the misery that prevailed within, nor of the savagery to which I would be subjected. Remember Dotheboys Hall, the hellish Yorkshire establishment prevailed over by the wicked, one-eyed Wackford Squeers in Charles Dickens's *Nicholas Nickleby*? This is the novel, set in the mid-1820s, in which Dickens attacks both the peculiarly English tradition of brutal boarding schools and the callous parents who consign their poor offspring to gross negligence, maggoty food and flea-ridden beds. My personal experience was not quite that awful, and my parents were by no means callous. They cared about me greatly, and wanted only the best for their son. Had they had any inkling of how horrendous my life within its walls was to be, I know that they would have reconsidered sending me there. They knew nothing, of course. I didn't tell them. I don't know why I didn't. Perhaps I feared that I wouldn't be believed. Yes, I think it was partly that, and also partly because I was so ashamed of some of the things that happened to me. Had they known the extent of the abuse that I suffered, I feel sure that they would have come immediately, and would have taken me home. Wouldn't they?

The thing that baffles me now is that corporal punishment was not only expected but acceptable. Teachers routinely attacked their pupils physically for the most minor offences, with a viciousness out of all proportion to the petty little 'crime'. There was something very sinister, something unthinkable, about the pleasure that these men appeared to derive from hurting boys. I find it hideous now that they were allowed to get away with it. In these infinitely more enlightened times, when corporal punishment itself is a crime, we know enough about child development and the long-lasting effects of the physical abuse of minors – spanking, beating and flogging, the cane, the slipper, the ruler and worse – to know that blind eyes must never again be turned. Our Headmaster, Charles Johnson, used to drive around the school grounds after dark in his snazzy Mark 8 Jaguar with the headlights on full-beam, trying to catch boys smoking. If he tracked you down, he'd be looking to expel you. It didn't put me off smoking. This, pre our understanding of cancer, was still a rite of passage, and one that I was not about to forego. I had a few little tricks up my sleeve to disguise this flagrant act of defiance, one of which was to take up my position next to the toaster in the music room. I didn't question it at the time, but have had occasion to do so since: what on earth was a toaster doing in the music room?

Looking back, which I find myself doing much more the older I grow, it alarms me to recall that the Head and his masters, evil though they seemed, were the least of our worries. The most fearsome sadists among us were in fact our own kind. I'm talking other pupils: older boys, many of them prefects, who would select the meekest and most 'punishable' little ones to be what we would nowadays call their gofers, their dogsbodies, their personal servants, taking care of their chores, making them endless cups of tea and shining their shoes. Those prefects and older boys would have had to go through all that when they themselves were years younger. This was now their time to have the 'favour' returned. Not that there was anything favourable about it. It was a system established originally to ensure the smooth running of boarding schools. Over the years it had spiralled out of control, but authorities had turned a blind eye. Senior boys, known as 'fag-masters', were supposed to care for their underlings and protect them from bullying. It must have been designed to relieve teachers of responsibility. But since as early as the 16th century, in top public schools such as Eton College, Winchester and St. Paul's, the system had been abused. Fags would be shouted deaf, beaten up and used as punchbags to alleviate anger and frustration. They would also frequently be molested, and used as toys for sexual gratification.

Buggery was an horrific daily occurrence. I have done my best to, but cannot forget, one particular older boy who went around pretending to be a prefect. He used his seniority to put the frighteners on the younger ones, coercing them into performing sex acts. I'm not quite sure how I managed to avoid what was so shockingly considered inevitable, but he never got me. Nor, I am thankful to report, did anyone else. I must have been blessed. I can't remember a single night, however when I retired to bed free from fear that some rogue might jump on me during the night and do something unspeakable.

It occurs to me only now that my parents must have known that I was more than likely to encounter and have to deal with this kind of thing. Why didn't they warn me about it? I don't suppose I could have expected my mother to take me aside and explain the ins and outs. But surely my father could have been a man, and have prepared me. The only excuse I can make on his behalf is that sex was such a no-go area in those days. It simply wasn't discussed. Mothers did not prime their bridal daughters before sending them off to the wedding-night barbarity of the marital mattress. Fathers would have run a mile rather than sit their sons down and talk them through the facts of life. We were a long way from our modern ability to discuss sex openly, without shame or embarrassment. We're talking regular, run-of-the-mill sex between a married, heterosexual couple. It's hardly surprising, then, that anything to do with homosexual activity, let alone male rape, was never referred to at all. It was hush-hush. It was still illegal, for a start. It would remain so for nearly a decade more. It might be hard to get our heads round now, but the maximum penalty for anal intercourse, which had been made a crime during the reign of Henry VIII, was life imprisonment. All other sexual acts between males had been declared criminal by Queen Victoria. Not until 1967, the year of the Beatles' *Sgt. Pepper's Lonely Hearts Club Band*, the Summer of Love, the launch of the first WEM P.A. system, the year that Marc Bolan launched Tyrannosaurus Rex, would private homosexual sex between two consenting males who had both reached the age of twenty-one be decriminalised, but even then not entirely throughout the land. Compare that to sixteen for sex between a man and a woman. I can't help wondering whether all those rapist prefects ever knew that they were breaking the law, and could have gone down for it. Presumably some sort of protection and exemption must have been assumed, because they were below the age of consent.

When I went home for exeats or during the holidays, nobody ever asked me whether anyone had tried to 'interfere with' me, as they called it back then. There were incidents, let's say, but I was big, and I managed to look after myself. I would have died rather than discuss it with my parents, in any case. I'm sure that most of us felt the same.

It was only a matter of time before the boy pretending to be a prefect was apprehended. I suppose the school had no choice but to make an example of him. The memory of his public shaming before the entire school hall is a most uncomfortable one. Fellow pupils were actually allowed to tear the boy's uniform off him, and to shred it in front of the rest of us. I can still see the look on his face, an unrepentant and unnerving leer. I don't remember the police turning up. I never heard about any parents being summoned. As far as I was aware, the school chose to deal with matters in-house, in its own peculiar way. Thinking about it now, the things they allowed boys to do to that fellow-pupil, a wretch though he was, were almost as bad as the things he had been doing to others. It made no sense, and it distresses me so to think of it. No school would get away with taking the law into its own hands nowadays. There are rules in place to protect both individual pupils and educational establishments from such things. Back then, boys found themselves trapped in this microcosm of the real world where they had only two choices: to fight back or be eaten alive. No wonder so many boys escaped and tried to run away. They were inevitably found, snivelling on the South Downs, and would be dragged back to prison to face the consequences. Which usually involved a ferocious beating and no food.

It wasn't all bad. My parents and sister would visit me sometimes, and take me out for the day to the seaside. Bognor Regis was nearby, a very pleasant resort, where we'd sit on the beach, paddle in the sea and eat ice cream. Sometimes we went to the pictures, to catch the latest film. One cinematic treat that sticks in my mind was *Ben Hur* starring Charlton Heston. Perhaps I identified with the slave who overcame. Perhaps I saw myself as a slave of sorts, in that godforsaken school. One of the worst aspects of my time there is that it must have cost my parents a fortune. They parted with it willingly, no doubt convinced that only the best was good enough for their son, and that they were lucky enough to be able to provide it. I miss my father and mother very much. How I wish I could have been open with them, and that I had been able to tell them the truth about how much I hated school. They are long-gone, of course. Would that I were able to tell them now.

Do I have any good memories at all? I do. A few. I recall with pleasure the visits to chapel for Eucharist on Sundays, after which we were permitted to go for walks. I remember taking part in sailing and canoeing ventures, both of which the *Boys' Own* boy in me was partial to. And of course, musicians will always find each other. I forged a firm friendship with a boy named Steve Hyer, the son of a rich German Jew with a penchant for fabulous cars, especially American ones. Steve had a white Höfner semi-acoustic which he played like a pro. He could out-strum me any day, he was by far the superior musician. He and I used to practise Duane Eddy numbers together for hours on end. We soon found ourselves a drummer by the name of Hallam, and were now as good as ready to tackle proper gigs. For some unfathomable reason – rock'n'roll was not considered desirable, not by any stretch; we were supposed to be into classical music, at the very worst, jazz – we were given permission to stage a few shows at the school itself. One of these almost incited the boys to riot. I can remember prefects standing in a row right in front of the stage like wardens at a football match, poised to take on and eject the rebels. A few teachers lurked about, taking it all in. Perhaps they secretly enjoyed it.

Other than these rare few musical interludes during which I got my chance to shine and took full advantage of it, I never distinguished myself significantly as a scholar. I was still the one with my head in the clouds rather than my nose in a book. I realise that this must have come as a huge disappointment to Mum and Dad, who would have had lofty expectations of me. I did all right at French, probably thanks to my dual heritage. It nudged me up a stream or two, to the annoyance of others. I was still good at Art, at least, which was something. I was also useful on the rugby pitch as a second row forward, or lock. The locks are the engine room of the scrum, and are usually the tallest and most powerful, with an acute sense of timing and wicked scrummage technique. I found the scrum a terrifying but thrilling head-to-head of shoulders, elbows, knees, feet and foreheads. Jaws jut, punches are thrown, and there prevails a sense of a pressure cooker about to blow at any moment. Which was the way I felt inside my head, much of the time. I did reach a stage at which the mildest taunt would provoke a pummelling from me for my tormentor. Angry young man was the size of it. There were things I'd never got over which got the better of me. I was quite a mild boy most of the time, but capable of losing it completely, which every now and again I did. Whoever it was who teased me rotten that I was in dire need of a girlfriend to calm me down, he was not far wrong.

But what to do about that? Ours was a single-sex school. Apart from the odd matron, nurse, secretary, teacher, and visits from mothers and sisters, we hapless lads were rarely exposed to females. In consequence, especially once puberty had kicked in, girls were the holy grail. We were obviously not that unusual in this regard. I became a sucker for screen goddesses, those luscious, luminous ladies who stared down at me in all loveliness. Boy oh boy, I couldn't get enough. Of them all, I fantasised most about raven-haired, violet-eyed Elizabeth Taylor, and took to taking her to bed with me each night. It was the ultimate safe sex. Back in the real world, during daylight hours, I wasn't nearly so proficient. My attempts at cool flirtatiousness with the sisters of school chums and local village girls were, I cringe to remember, clumsy and awkward. Not that it felt that way to me at the time. I was tall, blond, and considered to be 'good-looking', whatever that meant. I felt that I was doing rather well 'with girls', though curiously I always dumped them before they could dump me. That old devil called denial, that terrifying fear of rejection. Here they came, rearing their ugly heads again. Although surrounded by boys who had already 'gone all the way' with casual girlfriends, I didn't have the nerve to go there myself. I'd pluck up the courage to arrange a liaison, then find myself pulling out at the last minute, so to speak. I never had the courage to go through with it. It would be ages before I surrendered my virginity. What a relief and a half when it was done.

5

TEENAGE KICKS

You've got to be where the action is. That's another thing about boarding school: herding together a bunch of kids from similar, privileged backgrounds and cutting them off from the outside world in a relatively isolated location promotes an unhealthy, suspicious and toxic environment that hardly prepares you for real life. No wonder we go stir-crazy. To be trapped in a cauldron of heightened anxiety with everyone looking over his shoulder, and confined to contact with a limited range of humans, brings out the worst in people. I still think about it. It still bothers me.

I had not, unsurprisingly in the eyes of those with an interest, made the most of my time at Seaford. I emerged a resounding academic failure, poised to take full advantage of all that life was not about to throw at me. I certainly wouldn't be going to university or any equivalent establishment of tertiary education any time soon unless I could master the basics, would I. If I was going to make anything of myself and my life, it was put to me in no uncertain terms, I had no alternative but to knuckle down, do some actual revision for a change, and re-sit my exams. But where? Wild horses would not have got me back to boarding school.

My mind, of course, was on other things. Just as I was now fantasising about traversing the vast expanse of America and experiencing the even greater swathe of its diverse music first-hand as soon as I could scrape the fare together, I was also longing to be let loose in the music capital of the UK. I'd dipped a toe in once or twice previously with the odd excursion to 'the Smoke', as the capital was known during the Fifties on account of its filthy pea-souper fogs. I had managed to get out again unscathed. It now felt like high time to immerse myself. Right on cue, as if having read my mind, Dad seemed to wave a magic wand to get me there. Imagine my delight when he informed the family that we were moving yet again: this time to within spitting distance of Soho, the epicentre of London's music scene. That move was by no means for my benefit. Our father had decided that he no longer wanted to commute to work. He sold half our garden for development and spent the money on another house in Notting Hill. He had another new job, working for the Institute of Cancer Research at their Chester Beatty Institute in Chelsea. Founded in 1909, the Institute was and remains renowned throughout the world for its research into the link between smoking and lung cancer, for identifying carcinogens that damage DNA, and for the discovery, during the 1950s, of a number of important chemotherapy drugs. It would also, eventually, initiate the Cancer Genome Project. Dad had bought us what I considered to be a small, pokey house on Callcott Street, near Notting Hill Gate tube: a then state-of-the-art underground station which had recently been rebuilt, and which offered virtually instant access to all corners of London via the Central, District and Circle Lines. Five stops to the east and I could be in Oxford Circus, within a few minutes' walk of Leicester Square, Piccadilly Circus and Covent Garden. Three to the west and I'd be on the threshold of Shepherd's Bush. The Circle and District lines would whizz me directly north to Bayswater, Paddington and the Edgware Road. Round the other way, I had rapid access to Sloane Square, Victoria and the city of London. One of the greatest cities in the world was suddenly my oyster. The Swinging Sixties had kicked off in more ways than one.

Notting Hill was a peculiar place in those days. The Ladbroke Grove end was a depressing muddle of shabby old houses segmented into squats and cramped rented flats. It was the kind of area into which you wouldn't want to stray by yourself late at night. The neighbourhood comprising Elgin Crescent, All Saints Road, Blenheim Crescent and Arundel Gardens was equal parts hippie and upwardly-mobile. An unlikely blend, you might think, yet most of them seemed to be living side-by-side harmoniously enough. There were still bomb sites and vacant stretches where buildings had been demolished but not yet replaced; where gangs of barefoot children tore about, dodging the many bonfires. Most locals used the market during the week to buy their vegetables. On Saturdays, Portobello took on a different complexion altogether, when the hipsters flooded in to peruse the antique stalls and buy second-hand garb. The 'vintage' of our day was all from the Twenties and Thirties.

I have sometimes thought that the modern view of Notting Hill life back then is rather idealised. I hear it described as London's answer to hippie mecca Haight-Ashbury in San Francisco, or the Greenwich Village of the bohos in New York. They eulogise about it having been a hotbed of glamour, an intoxicating blend of musicians, fashionistas, artists, drug-dealers, cool down-and-outs and wild eccentrics, hanging around the stalls and the independent record shops. Two of the UK's most prominent record labels were founded there: Chris Blackwell's Island Records, and Richard Branson's Virgin. They bang on today about 'village life' there as if it had been all cosy country cottages with roses growing around the doors, where everyone knew everyone else, and where all were friendly together. But the area was not all it has been cracked up to be. A lot of lost people hung out there. It was an enclave for the victims of drug culture. Marijuana and LSD, known as acid, were the drugs of choice at that time. Heroin and cocaine would kick in during the Seventies, when alcohol experienced a resurgence too. No one looked each other in the eye or passed the time of day when they encountered others in the street. The prevailing mood was that the world was in a dreadful state, but who cared because we wouldn't be around much longer to watch it disintegrate. Plus ça change.

Our house sat on the north-west side of Camden Hill, a comparatively safe and desirable area that you'd part with millions to live in now. My parents found me a college not far away in Holland Park, where I could retake my exams. The regime was tough. The saving grace, I think, was art, which offset the misery of so much intense cramming. I started taking an art magazine called *The Studio*, and studied artistic trends. Sweeping changes were taking place in the art world, I knew, and I was keen to keep abreast of them. Everything caught my eye and sparked my imagination, from pop art to Francis Bacon.

I felt sorry for my sister Philippa, who had not wanted to leave her close friends in Reigate for the uncertainty of the big, bad city. Dad reassured her that we'd be keeping the Reigate house for the time being, and that we would spend weekends there as often as possible. Philly hated London. She was a country girl, and only thirteen. London wasn't for her. She was very clever, and had done well at school until then. But she could never come to terms with life in town after the freedom of open fields and riding horses. She would choose the life of a teacher in the end, and would relocate to Scotland.

My mother didn't seem to mind all the upheaval and to-ing and fro-ing, as long as she remained close to my dad. I think I was well aware, at that stage, that my father came first in her eyes, and that Philippa and I were less important. How, I reasoned with myself, could she possibly have left us otherwise? But she did, and there was always the threat that she would do it again. Big, strapping school-leaver with everything going for me and with my whole life ahead of me though I was, the fear still haunted me. Our house was an elegant Georgian terraced place. Two-and-a-half storeys. Compared to the spaciousness of our home in Reigate, all the rooms seemed ridiculously small. My father and I had to bend and mind our heads, in order to get through doorways. I did find it rather claustrophobic, and was probably quite rude about it. I kick myself with hindsight: most people would give anything to live in such a beautiful house in such a prime location now. My antidote to our cramped living conditions was to hit the streets and go wandering. I'd sometimes jump on the tube, or I'd simply walk for a mile or two, until I found myself in the edgy 'West Indian quarter', lured by the simmering, soothing sound of the steel drum. I had gleaned little from History lessons about the countries of the Commonwealth and the British Empire, or about the African-Caribbean immigrants who helped post-war Britain get back on her feet: the so-called Windrush Generation, named after the ship that conveyed the first contingent of immigrants here. Invited, and wanted, they came in search of opportunity, abundant work, a new life. What most of them got was ripped off and racially abused by reprobate landlords, attacked by young white fascists, and horribly victimised during the race riots of 1958. It makes me ashamed to think of it, how our country treated them. I liked the look of these people. I responded to their quiet, dignified demeanour. I loved the music they made.

★

Dad's solution to the problem of lack of space for us all at home in the evenings was to encourage me to attend a youth club in the massive crypt of the Brompton Oratory, a huge Roman Catholic church in Knightsbridge. I was all for it until I got there, when my nerves got the better of me. I felt like turning round and running straight back home. But I persevered, pretty soon realising that I was not the odd one out because everyone there was the odd one out. The youth-clubbers comprised all kinds, from slick Mods to leather-clad Rockers to crêpe-soled Teds. It welcomed all sorts, and anything went. The club had a band who played the usual covers of Shadows and Ventures numbers, as well as classic rock'n'roll hits. I stood against the wall during their performances and watched them intently. Would I ever have the courage to confess that I played too? This seemed a far cry from the tennis club gigs in Reigate or the random performances at school. But then came my opportunity, as opportunities always do if you wait long enough. I rocked up one night to discover that the show couldn't go on because the bass player had injured his hand. He'd be off-duty for the duration. The vicar asked about among us to see if anyone else could handle a bass guitar. I don't know what made me do it, but I found myself volunteering. I took to it easily: the bass has fewer strings. I practised the songs and I stepped up to do my bit. After that, there was no stopping me.

I soon found my feet at the youth club, and even made a couple of friends. One was Pete Hollis, another bass player like me. The other was Steve Gregory, an almost fully-fledged virtuoso musician, who had done time in his school orchestra and who was destined to study at London's Guildhall school of music, where he would excel in piano, guitar, clarinet and saxophone. The latter was his signature instrument. He would lend his skills down the decades to the recordings and live performances of Georgie Fame, Geno Washington and Fleetwood Mac. That's him on the Stones' 'Honky Tonk Women', and that's his sax solo on George Michael's 'Careless Whisper'. Steve was obviously going places. Before he did, he was just my pal down the youth club. We sat around talking, and he told me about a ballet studio on Latimer Road where he rehearsed with a few other musical like-minders. Why didn't I come down and join in? He didn't have to ask me twice. I remember looking over my shoulder every few minutes as I made my way along that down-and-out avenue, wondering what on earth I was doing in such a bleak part of the world and what in the world my mother would say. A middle-class boy on the frontline was a fish out of water, no mistake. Against the odds I made it, to an empty, mirrored studio with a scuffed wooden floor in which sat a lone pianist at an upright, playing brilliantly. The beauty of the music blew me away. When he noticed me, he stopped playing abruptly. I enthused, gormlessly, and he thanked me, before introducing himself. His name was Pete Bardens. We got talking, and sat around rapping about music for what seemed like hours. I remember nothing further about what happened that long afternoon, not even whether any other musicians put in an appearance. All I recall is meeting long-haired, long-faced Pete. I couldn't have realised at the time that our encounter would change my life.

Where do you start? He was everything I wished I was: a groovy London grammar-school boy who had grown up in the city and was well-versed in its foibles. He knew his way around. He had something about him, an eccentric style. He didn't try too hard to look like anyone else, he looked exactly like himself. He was a bit foppish, a bit of a peacock, and was confident, opinionated and cool. He was six months my senior, and a gifted musician, who would go on to become the keyboard player with Seventies cult prog-rock band Camel, from Guildford.

Pete and I had a couple of things in common. Music and extraordinary fathers, for a start. The details emerged little by little, as Pete and I got to know each other and spent more and more time hanging out together. His sweet, slightly pompous, chaotic and kaleidoscopic dad, Dennis, was an incorrigible womaniser and a boy-about-town. He blew his own trumpet shamelessly, but in a most appealing way. I loved going over to their house and listening to Dennis holding court. His stories were mesmerising. He had worked as a journalist and in Second World War espionage. He wrote novels, biographies of such luminaries as Churchill, Princess Margaret and prison reformer Elizabeth Fry, and books about ghosts and psychic phenomena. It didn't surprise me at all to learn that he had founded BBC television's current affairs programme *Panorama*, given that he was such a panoramic individual himself. His mother had abandoned the family when he was three years old, and had run off to Australia. He would survive both his wife and his son Pete to live to the ripe old age of ninety-two. God rest his soul, I adored him.

Pete and I sat around talking a good deal, mostly about music. We agreed that it had taken a funny turn lately. The Sixties hadn't exactly got off to a good start. Perhaps the industry was still reeling from the fallout of the day the music died: 3rd February 1959, when Buddy Holly, J.P. 'Big Bopper' Richardson and Ritchie Valens went down in a light aircraft close to Clear Lake, Iowa during a tour of the Midwest. Holly, only twenty-two, was already a star, thanks to his wholesome boy-next-door image, wizard guitar-playing and catchy tunes. Along with thousands of other wet-behind-the-ears youths, I had taught myself to play his songs 'Peggy Sue' and 'That'll Be the Day'. Valens, just seventeen, was on the up thanks to his hit 'Donna'. DJ and songwriter Richardson had made his mark with 'Chantilly Lace'. Two pregnant wives, Holly's and Richardson's, and a new bride, the pilot's, were widowed. Hearts around the world were broken. Why did the fateful date become known as 'the day the music died'? Because these three were among the last classic rock'n'rollers still standing. Little Richard had 'got God' and had pledged his troth to Gospel. Elvis had been drafted into the US Army, and would emerge a matinée idol. Chuck Berry, of 'Maybellene', 'Roll Over Beethoven' and 'Johnny B. Goode' fame, was a youthful armed-carjacker who grew up to be a paedophile porn addict and sexual fetishist with a penchant for spying on women in bathrooms. He was incarcerated for smuggling across state lines a fourteen-year-old Apache girl, who was arrested for prostitution soon afterwards. Eddie Cochran, 'James Dean with a guitar', was dead too, exterminated in a car crash near Chippenham, Bath at the age of twenty-one while touring the UK with fellow rocker Gene Vincent. The latter survived. As had Dion di Mucci and Waylon Jennings, who were supposed to have been with Buddy in the plane.

The Buddy/Big Bopper/Valens tragedy would inspire Don McLean's greatest hit, 1971's 'American Pie'. Its title is a reference to the 'American Dream'. Its chorus line 'This'll be the day that I die' is a nod to Buddy's own hit. A ballad about Don's great hero, rock'n'roll, teenage culture, the loss of youth and the death of Fifties and Sixties optimism, it references many fellow musicians. Bob Dylan, 'the Jester'; Pete Seeger and Joan Baez, 'the King and Queen of folk', and Elvis, the King of rock'n'roll; the Beatles: 'the Quartet'; Mick Jagger: 'Jack Flash'; 'I met a girl who sang the blues': is that you, Janis Joplin? These and other icons are captured for all time in its imagery. The song is now even the subject of whole university courses. All Don has ever said in response to questions about its meaning is, 'It means that I never have to work again if I don't want to.' But he did.

This horrible ending, looking back, seems almost to have marked the beginning of something else. Until then, the primary purpose of popular music was for dancing, specifically at 'sock hops' in the US: so-called because such prancing was so often performed in gymnasiums, where participants had to dance in stockinged feet to prevent damage to wooden floors. Hence the line in Don's song 'You both kicked off your shoes.' The 'sacred store' sold Fifties albums. The 'thorny crown' references not only the Crucifixion, but also the price of fame.

Nothing is ever as cut and dried as history tries to make it. It wasn't simply that rock'n'roll was now consolidating itself into a specific genre as the result of the fact that white Americans had been listening to, soaking up and performing 'black' music. Most of the musicians who attempted to play it fell somewhat short of being able to reproduce black R&B – perhaps because they just didn't have that elusive quality called 'soul'. But instead of rock'n'roll limping along as a woebegone white man's imitation of a thrilling original, it was evolving into a genre in its own right. This happened for a cocktail of reasons, not least the emergence of more diverse musicians, new methods of production, more modern equipment, and an infinitely broader reach. There is, among the chroniclers, a tendency to dismiss the late 1950s and early '60s as a no-man's-land of dry, uninspiring, manufactured music that was little more than rock'n'roll circling in a holding pattern until Sixties pop exploded and knocked us all for a dozen. In fact, it was a whole, brief, historic period in its own right. This was the era of New York's Brill Building, that hallowed songwriting factory where partnerships such as Carole King and Gerry Goffin, Ellie Greenwich and Jeff Barry churned out numbers that would become early pop classics and stand the test of time. Maybe because it was the age of the 'Girl Group' – the Chiffons, the Shangri-Las, the Shirelles, the Ronettes, with hits like 'One Fine Day', 'Leader of the Pack', 'Will You Love Me Tomorrow' and 'Be My Baby' – it didn't do a lot for me. I was unaware then, but would come to appreciate later, that this was also the period of the inexorable rise and escalating dominance of the songwriting producer, a significant new variation on the theme. These were the guys – and they were all guys – who created and crafted records rather than 'just songs'. They wrote for the voices, personalities and image of particular artists. They figured out arrangements, directed the studio session recordings, bossed everyone about and oversaw the entire process from start to finish. The effect that this new approach would have on the industry was to prove far-reaching.

So which artists *was* I listening to? Which of them were influencing *me*? Who was I trying to emulate? The now Cliff Richard-less Shadows retained the power to thrill me, I think mostly because they were British and therefore *ours*. Billy Fury was another one I looked up to. He was smouldering, sexy and Elvis-y. His plaintive voice had a curious warble that was incredibly more-ish. The arrangements on his records could get a bit schmaltzy and melodramatic, but were addictive. 'A Thousand Stars', 'Maybe Tomorrow', 'Half Way to Paradise': what wasn't to like? The former Ronnie Wycherley from Liverpool would wind up scoring twenty-four hits during the Sixties, as many as the Beatles, and was much underrated. The Tornados, featuring the magnificent Clem Cattini on the kit – one of the most prolific drummers in British recording history – and George Bellamy, dad of Muse's Matt, on rhythm guitar, were Billy's backing band for a year and a half between 1962 and 1963, scoring a hit of their own en route. 'Telstar', written and produced by Joe Meek, was a Number One in the UK and a chart-topper in the US in December 1962. It was the second British recording to conquer the American charts that year, 'Stranger on the Shore' by jazz clarinettist Acker Bilk being the first. That couldn't be his real name, could it? I wondered for years. As it turned out, it wasn't. Somerset-born Bernard Stanley Bilk was nicknamed 'Acker' for his friendly demeanour, the word being local slang for 'pal'. His haunting instrumental became the first Number One single in the US by a British recording artist since the new Billboard Hot 100 chart had begun.

Despite all that, I despaired of the pop charts overall at that point because they were clogged to the nines with crooners, the kind your mother might have swooned over. Pat Boone and Frankie Avalon were simply not my type. Neither was Mel 'the Velvet Fog' Tormé, a Russian-Jewish former child prodigy and teen idol with a sweet voice and perfect pitch, who had been writing songs since the age of thirteen and was best-known for what they still call 'The Christmas Song': the one that goes, 'Chestnuts roasting on an open fire, Jack Frost nipping at your nose…' which he had co-written in a 1945 Californian heatwave with fellow songwriter Bob Wells. Jotting down December images in an attempt to cool themselves off, they unwittingly created a massive cross-chart hit for Nat King Cole. Who wouldn't give their right arm to have come up with such a classic? Just the one. It's all it takes. But Mel and I were never on the same page. He was scornful of rock'n'roll, denouncing it as 'three-chord manure.' He must have seen the writing on the wall.

★

Back at the ranch, things were ticking along, smoothly for the most part with the odd dramatic hiccup to keep things sizzling. My mother was now working for the Red Cross, doing her bit. My father was as obsessed with his work as ever. He had also become prone to what we called his 'turbulent moments', when he would appear to have a complete meltdown and lose the plot. These came on out of the blue, and could be quite terrifying. He sometimes even went on the rampage. There were times when we had no choice but to lock him out of the house. From such a mild man, these mood swings could be quite frightening. We were an eccentric family to say the least, each of us drama queens in our peculiar ways. But we were, for the most part I'd have to say, fairly happy. My parents offloaded our old house in Reigate eventually, to purchase a small country retreat with a chapel in Westfield, near Rye, East Sussex. But I was at that stage in life at which the last thing a boy wants to do is retreat. The opposite. I wanted to immerse myself in the thick of London life, and avail myself of all that it had to offer. There were a couple of drawbacks: one, that I didn't have any money; two, that I couldn't yet drive. It was a burning ambition of mine to get on with it and pass my test so that I could get my hands on my father's Bentley and go cruising around town impressing women.

I had carried on legging it back to Reigate for a while, to take part in rugby matches. Those weekend excursions on the train were a welcome diversion at first. They kept me in touch with old friends and my former way of life. But it wasn't long before it dawned on me that I had changed. I was no longer like them. Those boys had become men, the kind of men who were an altogether different breed from the one I had now evolved into. They had grown big and strapping. They wore their copious ale consumption as blatant beer bellies, the way Shakespearian heroines flaunt their broken hearts on their sleeves. By contrast, I was slim and elongated. My muscles were not especially apparent. My hair fell below my shoulders and flopped over my face, just like Pete's. In short, the Londoners with whom I now hung about bore no resemblance whatsoever to the Surrey savages. Not very much time had passed since I'd felt like a fogey walking gingerly into the youth club that first painful time. But now I was a fish out of water whence I came. Imperceptibly, even to me, I'd moved on.

6

HADES

It's about seizing the day. Not that the hackneyed Latin aphorism actually means 'seize the day'. Sorry to disappoint you. That's a somewhat aggressive interpretation of the Roman poet Horace's true meaning, as recorded in his two-thousand-year-old *Odes*. The accepted, celebrated translation suggests the kind of every-man-for-himself stance and snatch-what-you-can attitude that usually involves sodding everybody else. That's not what the lyrical poet otherwise known as Quintus Horatius Flaccus was on about. His advice counselled a gentler approach. A gathering rather than a grabbing, much as one might pluck a pretty wild flower from a fragrant hedgerow. Don't go asking me to quote from old Horace's acerbic iambic poems or hexameter verses, either. It's all too long ago. Any shreds that I might have committed to memory in order to fail an exam or two are long dissolved in the acid lakes of time. Let's just leave it that we agree among ourselves never to breathe a word to Dame Judi Dench, who had 'Carpe Diem' tattooed on her wrist for her eighty-first birthday. In upper-case. A classic example, if ever there was one, of leaving things a bit late. Saving the best 'til last? Go on, then. I have always much preferred the positive spin.

Which brings me to the Beatles. What can I tell you that has not already been proclaimed for the past fifty years via millions of words in hundreds of languages, about the four young working-class Liverpudlians whose music changed the world? Many will scoff at such a statement. I was there to witness it. I know it's true. They maintain their singular place in popular culture because of the way in which they invaded the collective consciousness. This had never happened before, and has not happened since. It was partly about timing: music was poised for something brand-new in the post-Fifties, post-rock'n'roll world. It was partly about politics: President John F. Kennedy had been assassinated in November 1963, and America was bereft and in need of saviours. The group had done their 'ten thousand hours' and grafted their craft to perfection while in residence in Hamburg. Their personalities and irreverent backchat were significant: never before had the world been confronted and challenged by a quartet of cheeky chappies, British for sure but not respectful, deferential, speak-when-you're-spoken-to youngsters such as these. They were gobby, told it as it was, sent up everything, refused to conform, chewed gum and smoked cigarettes throughout press conferences, and did it all with irresistible banter, wit and charm, such disarming charm that they seduced even the naysayers. That they were physically attractive helped enormously, as did the fact that there was a Beatle for everyone: adorable Paul with the voice of an angel; mocking John with his razor tongue; doe-eyed George and rough-around-the-edges Ringo: the 'everyman' Beatle who was most like most of us, suggesting that if *he* could do it, almost anyone could. They wrote their own songs, the kind of instantly-familiar numbers that convinced us we'd been singing them all our lives, but which were fresh and new and exciting. They played their own instruments, both live on stage and in the studio. They had a young, go-getting manager, suave Brian Epstein, who boldly went where no pop manager had gone before, modelling himself to some extent on Elvis's mastermind 'Colonel' Tom Parker, learning on the job and taking risks. They had a producer, in EMI's George Martin, who was an accomplished musician himself; who took their raw material, encouraged and shaped it, who harnessed their imagination and processed it through the limited technology available at the time to create records the like of which had not been heard before. Thus were more guitars sold in more corners of the globe than at any other time before or since, as the youth of the world rose to emulate them. Along with millions of others, I awoke to my destiny. I was going to be a rock star too.

There was a fly in the ointment, however. I was still cramming to retake my exams. I was not at all surprised when Pete Bardens rocked up at my place, enthusing wildly that the 'time was right' and that there was this band we must join right away. He had it all worked out! Venues would soon be falling over themselves to book us, guaranteed! While I was thrilled at the thought, and delighted that he considered me to be good enough, my heart sank simultaneously. I knew my father would never allow it. The financial burden of my education demanded a reasonable return. No way could I balance the commitment of so much studying with all the travel, late nights and exhausting routine of being in a band.

No way was Pete taking no for an answer. He insisted that I accompany him to meet the band right away – a blues outfit calling themselves the Hamilton King Blues Messengers. They were named after their frontman, a guy who would 'blow my mind.' What choice did I have? I wanted to learn the blues more than anything.

The British R&B boom, now in full swing, owed much to musicians Cyril Davies and Alexis Korner. Cyril had launched his London Skiffle Club in 1955, which used to meet above the Round House pub at the corner of Soho's Wardour Street and Brewer Street on Thursday evenings. This metamorphosed into the London Blues and Barrel House, frequented by such musicians as future Kink Davey Graham, Long John Baldry and Ralph McTell. It also welcomed visiting American blues musicians introduced by jazz band leader and trombonist Chris Barber, with names like magic spells: Big Bill Broonzy, Sister Rosetta Tharpe, Memphis Slim and Otis 'Walking the Blues' Spann, a wizard blues pianist. Muddy Waters also performed there, marking the first time a musician playing electric guitar had done so.

Korner and Davies, inspired, started playing amplified instead of acoustic music themselves. They founded a band, Blues Incorporated, and in 1961 moved their residency out of Wardour Street and over to the Ealing Club at Ealing Broadway, West London, where they would be joined on stage by other musicians including Rod Stewart. Another young sprite who used to jump up and take the mic was a Portsmouth-born lad by the name of Paul Pond, who as P.P. Jones would perform duets with a lad calling himself Elmo Lewis. P.P. Jones metamorphosed into Paul Jones, vocalist and harmonica player with Manfred Mann, who would score an international hit with 'Do Wah Diddy Diddy' in 1964. Paul would go solo in 1966, carry on singing, take up acting, and in 1979 would found the Blues Band. He is, to this day, a member of the Manfreds: his original group's own tribute band. His favourite blues record remains Sonny Boy Williamson's quavering 1951 classic 'Mighty Long Time', and you can't say fairer than that. Elmo Lewis, who had been born Lewis Brian Hopkins Jones, the son of a piano teacher, a gifted multi-instrumentalist and father of four children by an array of women before his twenty-second birthday, restyled himself as Brian Jones and founded the Rolling Stones. He and Keith Richards begged Paul Jones to become their lead singer and frontman, but he turned them down. They had to make do with Mick Jagger. They later formed their own blues club in Brian's hometown, Cheltenham in Gloucestershire.

★

It was during the worst winter anybody could remember, 1962/63, that Pete dragged me by the hair through the snow and ice to meet Hamilton King. From memory, we found him at The Castle, a local boozer on the Harrow Road. I was nervous about the encounter, having no idea what to expect. Pete had given me a rough outline: Hamilton was a wild West Indian, he sang and played harmonica, and was also a drummer. He'd previously been in Dave Hunt's Blues Band. Rarely spoken of today, they were a respected outfit on the emerging British blues scene, of which Blues Incorporated, John Mayall's Bluesbreakers and Long John Baldry were among the stand-outs. Future Kink Ray Davies would also feature in Dave Hunt's line-up, with a significant diversion, to be revealed, en route. Much of the music these guys made was far ahead of its time. Electrified blues had become the thing, reviving the true roots of rock'n'roll. What an antidote this music was to the tinny Merseybeat clones and manufactured pop groups now flourishing like mould and dominating the charts.

I am so often asked: Why the blues? What was it about that genre in particular that captured my imagination? I suppose it was partly because it went against the grain. It was quintessentially American, and was not the kind of music your parents would like: always a bonus. It was thrilling and sensual. It got right under your skin and it lingered there, throbbing. You could feel its rhythms, dormant in your body, even while you were going about your day and running your errands. It wasn't just music, it consumed you like a fever. For me, a traditional, emotionally-stunted, socially-stilted public school boy, it confounded every aspect of the way I'd been brought up and educated. It represented freedom. I don't suppose I gave much thought at the time to the fact that this was the music of an oppressed race of people who had endured unthinkable pain and suffering, and had taught themselves to express that suffering through music. The revival of this old music rendered it new to us, something 'original' to make our own. Were we beginning to question our own society for its shortcomings, in subtle and subconscious ways? It's certainly possible.

Thrown in at the deep end and against the odds, I was a member of Hamilton King's mighty blues band. Who could have predicted this? I was beside myself. It wasn't happening, I was bound to be found out. Playing with Hamilton proved to be an extraordinary apprenticeship. I couldn't take my eyes off him, for a start. He was a big, immaculately-dressed bear in a suit and tie, porkpie hat and multi-coloured socks. He was warm and friendly. His wide, gleaming smile rarely left his face. He sang with evangelical frenzy and flair, and could play you right out of any drab Notting Hill pub and all the way to the Mississippi or even to heaven when he blew his harmonica. Which, it crossed my mind, might well have been the same place. He was a real blues man, the music ran in his blood and beamed right out of his soul. He wanted *me* in his band. I adored him.

So here we were: frontman Hamilton, Pete on piano, Alan Scott on drums and a lead guitarist whose name now escapes me. His replacement joined us in 1963, with a name I won't ever forget. It was Ray Davies: the very same who had once played alongside Hamilton in Dave Hunt's Blues Band, paying their dues at the Piccadilly Jazz Club in Soho's Ham Yard at the bottom of Great Windmill Street, now the location of the fabulously ritzy Ham Yard Hotel. This once shit-stained, cobbled courtyard boasted a long line of jazz clubs dating back to the 1940s. Way before Ronnie Scott unlocked his doors for business on Gerrard Street in 1959 (he relocated to Frith Street in 1965), and started lobbying the Musicians' Union with his friend and business partner, fellow saxophonist Pete King, to lift the blanket ban on visiting American jazzmen and agree a reciprocal deal, there was Club Eleven tucked away in Ham Yard. The 'Eleven' evolved into Cy Laurie's jazz joint in about 1952; was restyled as the Piccadilly Jazz

Club, and was re-invented again in 1961 as the Scene Club, owned by Ronan O'Rahilly, manager of Georgie Fame and Alexis Korner and soon to be the founder of offshore pirate station Radio Caroline. The Scene stole the show as Soho's go-to Mod hang-out, drawing stars and groovers in droves. The Beatles, the Stones, the Yardbirds and the Small Faces frequented it. The Animals performed there, as did the High Numbers, before they became the Who.

The baby-faced teenage DJ, expelled-boarding-schoolboy Guy Stephens, who was only a couple of years older than me, was destined to become a major figure in the British blues and beat booms of the 1960s. He played it all: blues, R&B, pop, ska and BlueBeat, and surf music. He majored in Stax and Motown. He was precocious, fascinating and given to self-contradiction. He founded and was president of the Chuck Berry Appreciation Society. His enthusiasm for such music had considerable bearing on Pye International's releases of records by Berry, Bo Diddley, Sonny Boy Williamson, Howlin' Wolf and the rest on the Chess label. Stephens paid Chuck Berry's bail, extracted him from jail and flew him to the UK for his first British tour in 1964, supported by the Animals, Carl Perkins and the Nashville Teens. Island Records' boss Chris Blackwell hired him to run the UK branch of American Juggy Murray's Sue record label that same year, and oversaw the release of hits by Ike and Tina Turner, Elmore James, Donnie Elbert, Rufus Thomas and more. Stephens obtained imports from Murray and from the heads of other US labels to play at Scene way ahead of everybody else, making the club an even more desirable destination. Chris Blackwell then encouraged him into record production. Guy cut his teeth on Alex Harvey, the Scottish rock and blues artist who rose to fame during the Seventies with the Sensational Alex Harvey Band. He became Island's head of A&R and was an inspiration to me, for reasons which will become apparent. He conjured Procol Harum, thought up their name, and suggested their magnum opus 'A Whiter Shade of Pale'. He also helped found, then named, produced and managed Mott the Hoople. He produced the Clash's knockout third album *London Calling*, which in 2003 would be ranked by *Rolling Stone* at Number Eight on their 500 Greatest Albums of All Time. He once said, 'There are only two Phil Spectors in the world... and I'm one of them!'

But Guy's story would not end well. An alcoholic and a depressive, he was imprisoned for drug possession, emerging to find that his entire record collection had been stolen. He suffered a breakdown, took an accidental overdose of the medication prescribed to help him overcome his alcohol dependency, and died in August 1981. He was thirty-eight.

★

Ray Davies was a shy, self-effacing type. He didn't say much, which was probably just as well, given that neither Pete nor Hamilton was reticent. There must have been all kinds of reasons for Ray's demeanour at that point in his life, before success and fame kicked in. It's futile to try and analyse a person in hindsight, and I'm no-one to judge. That he was a brilliant musician was enough. He was a secondary modern boy from North London's Muswell Hill, and had for some time been in a school band with his younger brother Dave, their bass-playing classmate friend Pete Quaife and drummer John Start. Calling themselves the Ray Davies Quartet, they specialised in Ventures and Shadows instrumentals and rock'n'roll classics. Ray began to explore London's R&B scene when he progressed to Hornsey Art College. It was how he found us. Dave Davies, meanwhile, continued as a trio with Quaife and Start as the Ramrods.

So many musicians came into the industry via art school that it could almost be said to be a pre-requisite. In his 1998 *New York Times* interview, David Bowie commented on the phenomenon:

'You know, twenty-five years ago there were a whole crop of us that tried to drag all the arts together and create this potpourri, a kind of new essence for English music,' he said. 'It started even before us, in the mid-Sixties, when so many of our blues players and rhythm & blues bands came out of art school. In Britain, there was always this joke that you went to art school to learn to play blues guitar.'

The joke was that David Bowie himself never actually attended art school. Whenever he referred, in later years, to his 'art-student' days, even citing 'Bromley School of Art' as his alma mater, he was, to put it nicely, rewriting history. He left school in 1963 at the age of sixteen with a single O Level, in Art. He then went straight out to work, landing a job as a trainee visualiser in a London studio while pushing on as a casual musician with his old school band, the Konrads. He later diversified, with his school friend turned bona fide art student George Underwood, as Dave's Red & Blues. Then it was the Hooker Brothers, the King Bees, the Lower Third, the Buzz, the Riot Squad, Davie Jones and the Manish Boys... and he got there in the end. But never to art college.

Bromley School of Art, incidentally, which dated back to 1878, became Bromley College of Art post-war, before David was old enough to have gone there. In 1959, still ahead of his time, the establishment merged with Beckenham School of Art's Department of Furniture Design, and relocated. In 1975 it moved again, and is today part of Ravensbourne University London. Their Wikipedia page lists Bowie as a 'notable alumnus'. Which he never was.

Still, we'll let him off, and will focus on those, including Ray, who were genuine art students: the likes of John Lennon: Liverpool College of Art; Keith Richards: Sidcup Art College; Vivian Stanshall and Larry Smith of the Bonzos: Central School of Art. Neil Innes went to Goldsmiths; Roger Ruskin-Spear to Ealing College of Art, as did Freddie Mercury and Pete Townshend; Pink Floyd founder Syd Barrett was at Camberwell School of Art; Roger Waters, Nick Mason and Richard Wright all attended the Regent Street Polytechnic, now Westminster University; Bryan Ferry studied Fine Art at the University of Newcastle, and worked as a ceramics teacher; Brian Eno graduated from Winchester School of Art. You can see where this is going.

Ray was an inspiration to me in so many ways. You could almost see creativity bubbling like boiling chocolate beneath his skin. He was always gagging to play, and was up for whatever Hamilton wanted us to try, from Howlin' Wolf's 'Smokestack Lightnin'' to Barrett Strong's 'Money'. Everything we did sounded fantastic to me. Ray was never less than right on it. We practised all over the place, wherever we were allowed to, which occasionally meant all of us cramming into my tiny box bedroom in our house on Callcott Street. All, that is, except the drummer, whom the neighbours would never have tolerated. We lifted the roof without him as it was. Every rehearsal felt like a proper gig. The collective energy we exuded felt like dynamite.

I learned so much from Ray, not least about cinema. I was more than familiar, like him, with the Roy Rogers pictures that were popular when we were kids. Unlike him, I'd never seen anything

X-rated. While James Bond flicks were all the rage, Ray was exploring Italian neo-realist movies and Japanese film maker Akira Kurosawa's groundbreaking samurai epics and social dramas. So-called 'New Waves' and convention-defying cinema began to overturn Hollywood glitz and fantasy to deliver real life to the silver screen. This was all a thrill for me. What I learned from Ray began to shape an alternative future. While my father was convinced that I could make it to the University of Cambridge to read Theology, I knew that I was destined for art school. Persuading him to allow me to go was going to be a challenge. My mother hated it when we raised our voices at each other, but our tempers got the better of us while we tried to work things out. In the end, we reached a compromise: that I could attend art college provided I play to my strengths and focus on the discipline of painting. In order to apply, I needed a portfolio of work. It was to this that I now turned the spare attention that I was not already devoting to my music. By my best efforts, including a painting of the London Underground, I won offers from both St. Martin's and Goldsmiths. I was seduced by the idea of the latter, but I had to be honest with myself: the schlep from Notting Hill all the way to New Cross and back every day would soon have defeated my lazy ass. I settled instead for the Byam Shaw School of Art, which was an independent college in those days. More importantly, it was only round the corner from home on Campden Street. It was about as far-removed from Ray's cool, progressive Hornsey college as you could get. The place was, literally, old-school: a throwback to 19th century Parisian establishments of the Beaux-Arts.

But I loved it so much that I found myself racing there each day, eager to get back among the easels and up to my elbows in paint. I adored hanging out with other artists, and immersing myself in all things Monet and Manet, Degas and Cezanne. The artist's life was perfectly up my street. I was pretty good at composition and still life. I was even better at life drawing, during which the odd erection from a life model, while it sent my more sensitive classmates scuttling, left me unfazed.

The icing on the cake was that Pete Bardens became a Byam Shaw boy too. I assumed that we were in for a fun few years there together, but alas, he didn't fall for the lifestyle the way I did. Not to put too fine a point on it, he hated it, and loafed around sending it up. He couldn't stand most of his fellow students, and denounced the female contingent as 'stuck-up debs.' He had a point. They were mostly rather posh and proper, and would only date boys whom Mummy and Daddy might consider to be marriage material. Even with my background, I barely stood a chance, so poor Pete was on a hiding to nothing. Years later, when I read biographies of the Beatles and learned that John Lennon had squandered his school days filling his own newspaper 'The Daily Howl' with vicious caricatures and spiteful damnations of his teachers, I was reminded instantly of Pete. His own wicked sketches and malicious cartoons did little to impress our tutors. His tenure at Byam Shaw was short-lived.

I managed to last a little longer there than Pete. But all too soon, with the nation and soon the whole world in the grip of Beatlemania, the lure of the rock'n'roll lifestyle proved too great. I surrendered myself completely to Hamilton King, and to the business of making music. Which meant heading on down to Soho – specifically to Gerrard Street.

Most of the throng milling along it now have little inkling of what Gerrard Street was like in those days. The pedestrianised main thoroughfare of London's Chinatown, attracting more than 17 million tourists a year during pandemic-free times, is crammed with Chinese restaurants, supermarkets and tat shops, and strung year-round with scarlet New-Year lanterns. There is a jolly, party atmosphere about it now. But back in the early Sixties it was one of the most dangerous drags in the capital. Chinatown had begun to flourish there when Chinese sailors and their families moved inwards from their original settlement of Limehouse in the East End, after the slums there were cleansed during the 1930s and then bombed during the 1940s. They were attracted by affordable short-term rents, and wasted no time in establishing their kitchens, retail businesses and gambling dens. By the time I started hanging out there, its dank underbelly was a labyrinth of brothels, seedy nightclubs and sleazy shops selling the types of magazines and books that had to be carried away in plain brown paper bags. Most of its restaurants were shabby places past their prime. Peter Mario's, one of the more decent joints, specialised in Anglicised Italian fare and boasted two famous customers, one being 'Our 'Enery', heavyweight boxer Henry Cooper, who had represented Britain in the 1952 Olympics, and who would fight Muhammad

Ali twice while the latter was still Cassius Clay. Henry was in there so often that he married one of the waitresses, a pint-sized beauty from northern Italy called Albina Genepri. Mario's other celebrated customer was a violent criminal by the name of Billy Hill, who had stabbed his first victim when he was fourteen years old, had been a black-market racketeer during the War, mentored the Kray Twins, and was now involved in the relieving of aristocrats of their fortunes at top-notch gambling clubs. He ran his smuggling, armed robbery and protection-racket empire from his restaurant table. It used to put the fear of God into me, just walking past. The street was also home to a number of rough and ready studios that supplied the kind of photos to be found in the aforementioned books and magazines.

★

Our band began to rehearse regularly in one of those seedy Gerrard Street clubs. It was called The Kaleidoscope. You ran the gauntlet to get there. I sometimes find myself trying to imagine what the last village in central London was like before the rot set in. Sweet images flood my brain, of a place reminiscent of a pantomime set or a medieval street scene. It's a quaint little neighbourhood; a place with pleasant open spaces for promenading and passing the time of day: Soho Square and Leicester Square. Friendly butchers, bakers, fishmongers, cheesemongers, deli-owners, tailors, clock- and last-makers trade busily. The theatres, pubs and family-run restaurants are already old. Those born in Soho, and who had lived there all their lives, were being forced out by undesirable newcomers. Come the early Sixties it had become a fully-fledged red-light district, a place of sex shops, strip joints and hookers lingering in doorways as they waited to pick up tricks. Street corners all the way down to the steps of the Eros statue in Piccadilly Circus were crammed nightly with pimps, card sharks and drug dealers. Venues such as Paul Raymond's Revue Bar and the Windmill Theatre flashed their erotic wares with neon signs. By the Eighties, Soho would be overflowing with topless bars, fully-nude shows, porn shops, saunas and massage parlours. It would eventually be cleaned up and regenerated. For now, it was Hades.

Yet there was something about Soho. Something so vital and seductive that I could not resist its allure. I often had to pick my way past punch-ups and knife fights as I edged along its busy streets to reach my destination in one piece. Mum and Dad would have had a fit, had they known. I'm sure they would have grounded me on the spot, finding it unthinkable that their mollycoddled, well-bred only son and heir was losing himself to the underworld. Needless to say, therefore, I told them as little as I could get away with. I was deliberately vague when questioned about where I was going, who with, what for, what time I would be back. As far as I was concerned, I was exactly where I needed to be at that moment in my life: down among the rock'n'rollers, the mods, the greasers, the beatniks, the radicals and the intellectuals, the racketeers and the robbers, the strippers and the strumpets, the unwashed eccentrics, the chess-players, cripples and threadbare heroes, the hustlers and the fortune-tellers, the dandies, the drunks, the drifters and the down-and-outs, at the throbbing heart of the nation's musical explosion, ready to leap when opportunity knocked. Soho was sex, drugs and rock'n'roll, and I was part of it.

There I'd go a-wandering, from the Bar Italia coffee shop on Frith Street to The 2i's on Old Compton Street – now Green-Plaqued as the birthplace of British rock'n'roll and reinvented as a fish and chip shop – where fledgling artists performed in its dank cellar and got picked up by a talent scout if they were lucky. My mind was buzzed in those places by superior types who carried the right books and dropped names like Jean-Paul Sartre, Simone de Beauvoir and Albert Camus, spouting existential musings as they drank the same coffee as us at the same Formica tables. Via jukeboxes newly-installed therein, I discovered new music, Bob Dylan in particular. The cryptic twenty-one-year-old poet with his head in the clouds and one eye on the nuclear bomb was the pin-up of the counterculture. His records, such as 'A Hard Rain's a-Gonna Fall', made a huge impression on me, as on millions of others. Dylan would write, in his 2004 memoir *Chronicles: Volume One*, about the inspiration for that song having been his spell spent researching newspapers on microfiche at the New York Public Library: 'After a while, you become aware of nothing but a culture of feeling, of black days, of schism, evil for evil, the common destiny of the human being getting thrown off course. It's all one long funeral song.' 'Blowin' in the Wind' was the answer, my friend. It got us talking about the Civil Rights movement. It got us talking about the artist himself. Where were we when he'd dropped in on London only months earlier, during that worst winter anybody could remember? He had come to star in a BBC play, *The Madhouse*. He had visited the same music stores we ourselves frequented, such as Dobells Folk and Jazz record store on Charing Cross Road. He'd slurped a black-no-sugar in Earl's Court's Troubadour coffee shop, where I myself had played with Hamilton King. Routine places and activities suddenly acquired new meaning, as if they had been blessed. We regarded the mundanities of our existence with new eyes. The man had moved among us, if only we'd known about it. It was like following in Jesus's footsteps, pretty much.

★

We played The Kaleidoscope often, as well as The Roaring Twenties on Carnaby Street and The Scene on Ham Yard. I loved The Scene, it was the coolest of the lot, with padded walls and cushions and a lounge-like atmosphere. Most of the crop-haired hipsters would be dressed in bum-freezer blazers and Sta Prest trousers, worn above the ankle to reveal snazzy socks and winkle-picker shoes. That was just the men. The girls were even more glamorous, their lipstick, eyeliner, beehives, bouffants and bobs making them look like movie stars. Gauloises-puffing clubbers came in all colours. There were no racial divisions, which reflected our line-up perfectly: a white band with a black front-man. We were all aware that interracial mingling was still frowned upon in some quarters. But music is colour-blind. We knew that undercover police lurked among us, keeping an eye and a nostril on the drug-users.

I was late to the party on that score. A lot of hot coffee and the occasional slug of booze were more than enough to keep me fizzing. It hadn't yet occurred to me to try anything else. I remember feeling quite shocked and fearful when we discovered someone's stash of marijuana inside one of our amps at The Kaleidoscope. To this day, I have no idea who was hiding it there, nor who was smoking it. All I cared about was whether we were going to get done for it. We didn't. The drug scene down at The Scene was somewhat more sophisticated. Amphetamines were the name of the game: the French Blues and Purple Hearts that were easily concealed in an inside pocket, down a sock or up a folded sleeve, and which would keep you up and at it for hours on end. But I didn't dare risk it. Not yet. Gigging by night and submitting to art classes by day, the last thing I needed was anything chemical messing with my brain.

I think my parents must have realised by then that my days at the Byam Shaw were numbered. My love of art had been eclipsed by my obsession with rock'n'roll. Mum and Dad were not best pleased. Their dreams for me were about to be dashed. I was too enthralled with what I was doing to let all the arguing and pleading get to me. Being in the Blues Messengers was all that mattered. We were building a considerable repertoire, including a swaggering, sexy Hamilton original called 'I Wanna Live'. It was the perfect showcase for our frontman's bluesy harmonica and roof-lifting vocals.

I had a girlfriend by this time, did I mention? I met her at Pete's house. I went round there one night to hang out, and he shouted down to say he was in the bathroom. I went up to find the last thing I was expecting: a beautiful girl shampooing his hair. So *this* was what being in a band was all about. Lucky for me, they were Just Good Friends. Her name was Sue Rowland, she was half-Jewish and she came from Hendon. She took a shine to me that didn't involve combs or conditioner. She was studying Fine Art at City & Guilds, so we had a head start. Lovely Sue glued herself to me, and took to accompanying me to all our gigs, quite often to rehearsals too. She adored the Blues Messengers, and would sit there transfixed by the sun that shone out of us. It wasn't long before I surrendered my virginity, relieved to get it over and done with but also that it happened with a girl as gorgeous as her. First love was true love, of course. Always is. I was in no doubt that I had found The One and that we would be together forever.

Did she go with me to my first and last recording session with Hamilton King? I can't remember. The significance of the occasion has obliterated all else. I was now a recording artist! We gathered at IBC Studios at 35 Portland Place, where Lonnie Donegan laid down 'My Old Man's a Dustman' and where the Kinks committed 'You Really Got Me' to tape. The Who's rock opera *Tommy* would be recorded there a few years later. Many a superstar passed through its doors, from the Beatles and the Bee Gees to Duane Eddy and Elton John. We recorded Hamilton's 'I Wanna Live' that day, together with a catchy Bo Diddley-esque number, 'Not Until', written by Johnny Kidd and the Pirates' lead guitarist Alan Caddy and singer Don Charles. How did we do? Rumour has it the Blues Messengers rose without trace.

7

ALL DAY AND ALL OF THE NIGHT

We paid our dues, jumping whenever our name was called to support acts and artists with a superior reputation. We were thrilled to be asked to open for Georgie Fame and his Blue Flames at The Flamingo Club on Soho's Wardour Street. Georgie, a Lancashire lad born Clive Powell, would become the only British artist to score three Number Ones with his only Top Ten chart entries: 'Yeh Yeh' in 1964, 'Get Away' two years later, and 'The Ballad of Bonnie and Clyde', written by Mitch Murray and Peter Callander, in 1967. He used to be Billy Fury's pianist, and had acquired some records from black American GIs visiting the club, including 'Green Onions' by Booker T. & the M.G.'s and Jimmy Smith's 'Midnight Special', both of which boasted the Hammond organ sound. These records inspired Georgie to get a Hammond organ of his own. The moment Pete Bardens saw the instrument in the flesh, having been seduced by its tones and versatility from listening to Jimmy Smith, one of his own heroes, he was determined to own one too. His wish was soon fulfilled, and of course Pete was ace on it.

Ray Davies was also hitting his stride. Although he still tended to be shy away from the spotlight, his on-stage confidence was growing all the time. I could barely believe it the first time he fell to the floor and started rolling around in front of us, kicking his legs in the air, playing his guitar behind his back and with his teeth, long before we ever witnessed Jimi Hendrix doing it. Even more surprisingly, he came out as a singer and began to take lead vocals on a few numbers. It dawned on me that, as much as he liked and respected him, Ray wasn't going to play second fiddle to Hamilton for much longer. He was clearly ready to strike out by himself, and to front his own band. One night, out of the blue, he crouched down on the pavement in front of us, holding his head in hands. All too soon he was back with his flamboyant and crazed lead guitar-playing brother. They replaced John Start with ex-Rolling Stone drummer Mick Avory and relaunched themselves as the Boll-Weevils and the Ravens, before restyling themselves the Kinks. Their frenzied, Beatles-inspired 1964 debut '45 for Pye, 'Long Tall Sally', was notable for Ray's wild harmonica and for its assured B-side, 'I Took My Baby Home.' With their third single that August, 'You Really Got Me', they struck gold. Good luck to them. But this was the beginning of the end for the Blues Messengers.

I took the news that Pete was quitting much harder. It was he who had introduced me to the band in the first place. I could barely believe it when he turned up in a dapper brown suit and announced that he was now managing the Senders, a group featuring my old youth club compadre Pete Hollis on bass and a guy called Eddie Lynch on vocals and guitar. I couldn't for the life of me see it lasting. Nor did it. He was a musician, for Pete's sake, not a manager. It wasn't long before he was jumping on stage, joining his charges on piano, becoming a fully-fledged member of the band, and even singing. All they needed now was a drummer.

It was at about the same time that Pete became aware of someone bashing the life out of a drum kit in the mews where he lived. Who was *this* arsehole doing their damnedest to wake the dead? Pete felt compelled to go and investigate. He found the culprit in a garage about three doors down from his place: a gigantic, somewhat unkempt-looking individual who introduced himself as Mick Fleetwood. The Cornish-born public schoolboy, son of a fighter pilot and RAF Wing Commander, had come to London to stay with his sister and her art-dealer husband. He had a proper job, in the accounts department of the Liberty department store in Soho. But Mick was never destined to spend his working life in retail. His boredom threshold was low, and he'd soon start letting his hair down. He grew it long and wild, and swapped sober office-style attire for a beatnik look. He later jumped on the hippie bandwagon, sporting the goblin boots, trailing cardigans and hipster flares. What he wore was almost irrelevant. He was a sight for sore eyes because he was huge. In any case, nobody cares what you look like when you can play drums like that. Pete was beside himself, as though he'd just discovered the Holy Grail in the spare-bedroom wardrobe. He wasted no time in inviting Mick to join the Senders.

His first outing with the band took place at a local church youth club. They played the usual old Shadows covers. I remember meeting Mick for the first time, perhaps it was even that night, and knowing that we'd be friends for life. We spoke the same language, which was basically music. We fell in together. Like Pete, he was soon a welcome fixture at my mother's table. She adored Mick. She must have done, to have turned a blind eye and ear to his constant tapping, rapping and drilling on every available surface, even with his knife and fork on his placemat during a meal. Neither Mum nor Dad would have put up with that kind of behaviour from me. It was as if they understood that Mick was a born thumper. He couldn't help himself. Every aspect of existence required a beat, and that was that. He'd drum-roll almost everything he came into contact with.

★

While I did still play with Hamilton from time to time, I was now in demand. Invitations to play bass flooded in, and some were out of the ordinary to say the least. One was with Steve Gregory, my old pal from the Brompton Oratory youth club, he who would soon lend his superlative sax-playing to 'Honky Tonk Women' and 'Careless Whisper'. The gig was at a joint called The Brush and Palette in Queensway. How to describe it? Imagine a strip joint crossed with a life-drawing class and you might get the picture: basically a sleazy strip show disguised as an art tableau. A bevy of sexily-clad lovelies would undulate onto the stage while the band banged out old R&B the likes of the Clovers' early 1950s hit 'One Mint Julep'. The models peeled off their clothes while the customers sat sketching them. I'm not sure how I managed to stay focused on the job in hand, surrounded as I was by gloriously abandoned nakedness. But they weren't all like that. Bands were mushrooming all over London and around the UK, providing endless opportunities for session guys like me: they always needed bass players and drummers. At one point I found myself playing for a guy called Leo Mason in his band the Booker T's, clearly a rip-off of the front man of the M.G.'s. And I became part of semi-pro line-up Fingernail Five, with the future abstract painter Ralph Freeman.

Fingernail Five were going places. We must have been, we had a manager. If you liked him, John Scott was your typical sharp-suited, fake tan-faced, tough-talking Svengali. If you didn't, he was a spiv. He meant business. He suffered no fools. He wheeled, dealt, and pushed his acts for gigs all over this land. Larry Parnes, the original rock'n'roll manager and concert promoter also known as 'Mr Parnes, Shillings and Pence' and 'the manager who turned down the Beatles', was John's role model. What Larry had done for early teen idols Tommy Hicks, Reg Patterson, Ron Wycherley, Clive Powell and the rest, reinventing them as Tommy Steele, Marty Wilde, Billy Fury and Georgie Fame respectively, John Scott was going to do for us. He wasn't quite *all* talk, but mostly. I soon grew disillusioned by him, just as I began to feel about life in general. Reality failed to live up to expectation.

Although I knew in my heart of hearts that Fingernail Five were not heading for the big time, we surrendered to the task and got on with the job. John got us the gigs, we played them, he banked his hefty percentage. We banged out R&B covers at air force base bashes, at debutante balls, at basically any venue that would book us. We saw little reward for our efforts, but we did see Great Britain in all its glory from the back of a Bedford van. The band inevitably fell by the wayside, but I wasn't too fussed. Decent bass players were always in demand, so I was rarely out of session work. I even threw my lot in with Tony Colton's brassy Big Boss Band at one point. Tony was a percussionist and singer from Tunbridge Wells. His name will be known to Yes fans, as he went on to produce for them, but he had his own moment in the spotlight as an artist and songwriter. Worth seeking out is his 'I Stand Accused', a Pye single in 1965. 'I've Laid Some Down in my Time' was a '66 Mod classic. He became a member of Heads Hands & Feet with Albert Lee and Chas Hodges – the latter later of Chas 'n' Dave fame; he co-wrote 'Negotiations in Soho Square' for the Tremeloes in 1967, 'Did it Rain' for Don Everly in 1974; co-wrote, with Albert Lee and Ray Smith, the gravity-defying 'Country Boy', and worked with Zoot Money, Shotgun Express and many others. A forgotten name with an illustrious history: aren't so many, in our game.

I came crawling in at all hours, and was getting home later and later from gigs. Mum and Dad were growing more and more exasperated.

They didn't have to look to know that my college work was suffering. I was eventually pulled up by the Principal of the Byam Shaw and issued with an ultimatum. It was time to choose: rock 'n' roll or art. While I couldn't give up music, I was reluctant to drop out of college and break my parents' hearts. They had done so much to secure me an education, despite my shortcomings. The least I could do was honour the commitment and finish what I'd started. I went through my pile of life drawings and with Ralph Freeman's help managed to scrape together a portfolio that just about saved me from the chop. I was able to breathe a sigh of relief, but only for the briefest moment.

If only I'd savoured that miniscule problem, and had milked it while I had the chance. I had no idea of the shit that was about to hit the fan when I went up to our communal Notting Hill roof garden with my girlfriend one starry, starry night soon afterwards. There we stood, hand in hand, gazing out across the spectacular London skyline. It was an exquisitely romantic moment, and all felt so right with the world. I was a teenager in love with this beautiful creature who had eyes only for me, and I was looking forward to a glittering future as a rock star. Not just any old rock star but the best kind, one who had graduated from art school. What could possibly go wrong?

It was Sue who brought me back to earth with a bump. Literally. Invited to admire the abundance of her breasts, it was drawn to my attention that they had grown larger. Significantly larger. This expansion, she explained, could mean only one thing. We were expecting a baby. We were seventeen. We thought we should elope.

8

MAN OF THE WORLD

She bottled.

Telling the parents is the hardest thing. All I could do was get it over and done with. My mother sat in silence as my father interrogated me. How on earth could this have happened? Well, you know. Did we both want to keep the baby? I didn't know. At which point my father stared at me as though I'd just crawled out of a bin. Did I want to spend my life as a petrol pump attendant? What was that supposed to mean?

I knew too well, of course, and I was shocked. Did it have to boil down to money and status? Was he really warning me that I'd be throwing my life away by becoming a gymslip father? I was disappointed in Dad – for the first time, I think. It must have showed. He had spent my lifetime drumming socialist principles into me while maintaining a second home, buying Bentleys and forking out for a toff's education. He was clearly socialist only to a point, or he wouldn't have poured scorn on humble employment. 'All work is worthy work,' he had always maintained. What, all work was equal, only some work was now more equal than other work? I was confused. I tried to see things his way. Despite my anger, it felt important to keep my parents onside.

What next? The all-embarrassing crisis meeting with my girlfriend's parents, at their place in Hendon. Where they didn't exactly blow me kisses at the gate or welcome me like their long-lost son. I was amazed, to be honest, that they even let me over the threshold. But there were three of us and there were three of them, and nobody wants a stand-off on their own doorstep.

Few silences have ever been more awkward. I forget who broke the ice, but the conversation soon became pretty animated. It was as if Sue and I were invisible. The adults talked over our heads. We weren't given any say in the matter, and were completely ignored. It was unthinkable, out of the question, that we should be 'allowed' to keep our baby. Although the word 'abortion' was not uttered – the procedure was still illegal in those days – it was obvious that this was what they were pushing for. All were in agreement, and that was that. Sue and I were never to see each other again. We were shocked by their draconian reaction, but helpless to do anything other than accept it. I felt crushed and ashamed. I know that she did too. I also felt very strongly that I wanted our baby to be born. At the time I was powerless to protest, but the horror of what was happening would have far-reaching consequences. It was only when I found myself in a stable marriage which brought forth three wonderful children that I was hit by the full impact of having aborted a child. What would he or she have been like? Would the baby have looked like me or Sue? Would he or she have been musical or artistic, or have been blessed with a blend of our strengths? It wasn't the baby's fault. Our son or daughter should have been allowed to be born, and to have lived out his or her life. The guilt weighed very heavily on me at that time in my life, as did the sense of loss. I'm sure that it must have been the same for Sue. Perhaps even more so, given that it was her body that was violated. I'd be lying if I said that I wasn't at least partly relieved at the time, in some ways. I was henceforth free to go on with my life and to continue unencumbered by responsibility for which I clearly wasn't ready. But I continued to wonder about that poor little child for a long time.

Thus was the first love of my life taken away from me. Though the thought of never seeing her again was at first unbearable, I did get used to it. There eventually came a time when I could no longer remember her face or her touch, and found myself wondering whether the relationship had actually happened. Which is not to say that I wasn't changed as well as chastened by the experience. There prevailed a sense, at home, that my family were no longer proud of me. I had let the side down, and had brought shame on the clan. I'm sure I didn't imagine that nobody looked me in the eye any longer, and that our family conversations were no longer the upbeat, lively discussions they had once been. It wasn't quite hell, but it was certainly purgatory.

When summer arrived, it was thought best that I should be despatched abroad for the duration. Out of sight, out of mind. They wanted rid of me. The sight of me was a daily reminder of something by which the whole family felt diminished. I could see their problem. The father of an old school friend of mine called Richard Borchard owned a liner shipping company, one of the oldest in Europe, which had been operating in and around the Mediterranean since the 19th century. The family invited me along for a cruise. It was precisely the escape I needed: from London, from my miserable family, and from the shame of what I had done. Only we don't leave our problems behind, do we. We take them with us wherever we go. There is no such thing as escape, and there is no absolution, because all the pain and sorrow we experience resides in our hearts.

We set sail from Tilbury Docks. The further away I got from home, the more I found myself thinking about Sue. How was she? *Where* was she? How was her health? How was she feeling mentally? Did she miss me at all, or had she put me out of her mind? It felt hideously unfair to me that I was swanning around the Med while she was being forced to endure the awfulness of an abortion. I could barely bring myself to imagine what she was going through. Would it hurt? Would she be scarred for life at such a tender age? Would it render her incapable of having more children? I could do nothing to help her, and I despaired. There was no getting away from it all, as I spent most of my time contemplating the hopelessness of it all. I also thought about chucking myself over the side.

This desperate stance was dramatically at odds with the life and soul of the party that I turned into when in the company of my friend and the ship's captain. I listened intently at dinner, and asked what I believed to be intelligent questions. I tried my damnedest to distract myself. I enthused wildly as we approached each successive port. The Rock of Gibraltar seen from the sea was 'mighty', and the Maltese coastline 'inviting'. What on earth was I on about? Everything looks glamorous from a distance, of course, the detail blurred by sun and shadows. Point-blank reality is always a wake-up call. I was no fan of the legions of cockroaches that swarmed over our Maltese bedroom floors. From Valletta Grand Harbour, my friend and I caught another boat to Palermo on the North coast of Sicily. Pausing to visit the magnificent church of Saint Catherine on the Piazza Bellini, we took a ferry to the mainland and set off on a journey up through Italy, in the direction of Pisa and Rome. I saw so much, but was moved by so little. That magnificent, eye-opening summer was mostly lost on me. I was going through the motions. My mind and my heart were on other things. I remember one day making the ludicrous mistake of treating myself to a shiny new Italian suit, the kind of thing I would never wear and the purchase of which I regretted immediately. But I couldn't be bothered to take it back. I lugged it with me onto a sleeper train bound for Paris, landing at the Gare de Lyon about twelve hours later. Another train to Calais, a packed Channel ferry to Dover and one last, drab commuter train into Victoria Station and I was right back where I'd started, still gasping beneath the weight of the problems I had supposedly gone away to escape. I had still lost the love of my life. I'd still let everyone down. They were all still miserable. So was I.

There was only one thing for it. Music had seen me through hard times before. Would it prove my salvation again? There was but one way to find out. It was back to the action. Just before I'd left on my pointless voyage, I had gone down to see Mick Fleetwood's and Pete Bardens's new group the Cheynes playing at Soho's Mandrake Club on Meard Street. They'd been building a good reputation, and were now billed as an R&B outfit to watch. They were a sight for sore eyes all right, got up in their bright shirts, sleek pants and Beatle boots, especially lanky Mick with his interminable legs. Their set was a wild, infectious blend of Buddy Holly, Bo Diddley and Little Richard interspersed with their own startling offerings. It was thrilling. *This* was the way to leave your woes behind. I dived in head-first.

I loved the Mandrake. It was just the right level of dingy while managing to stop short of sleazy. Its trio of sparse, wood-panelled basement rooms were open all-hours, and drew heaving crowds. When the place was packed, it was scorching. I couldn't help envying Mick and Pete as I watched them perform, and applauded along with the throng. They were doing exactly what I should be doing. This was really cool stuff, the genuine article. No dreary deb dances and sordid strip joints for these guys, this was a proper music venue with a discerning clientele. The Cheynes were slick and professional. They had a hard, blues-influenced sound, and played up a storm. They more than looked the part. A one-eyed blind man could have seen that they were going places. They'd landed themselves a deal with EMI's Columbia label. They had played Liverpool's Cavern Club as 'London's answer to the Beatles'. They had already released their debut single: a cover of the Isley Brothers' 'Respectable', in November 1963. I remember the first time I heard it, I was utterly gobsmacked. This was class. This was action. This was where I was supposed to be. There was a vivaciousness about their sound, about Pete's manic organ-playing and Mick's tempestuous drumming. There was even a Pete Hollis original on the B-side, 'It's Going To Happen To You,' which I found even *more* catchy, even *more* pacey, and so fantastically assured. It was as though they had been doing this stuff for years. And then the pennies dropped. If my friends were making a go of it, there was no reason why I shouldn't too.

But there was no sure-fire route to success. Not even with their talent. 'Respectable' flopped. They barely flinched. They could weather it, things were happening for them. A minor set-back like that did little to compromise their inclusion in a 'Group Scene' UK tour, during which they found themselves on the same bill as the Swinging Blue Jeans, Dave Berry and the Cruisers and Marty Wilde and the Wildcats, all supporting headliners the Rolling Stones and America's Ronettes. The Cheynes also served as the Ronettes' backing band for the entire tour.

The Stones, now the hottest band around, were the first to eclipse the Beatles. As the Fab Four's nemesis, they had found their niche. Mick Fleetwood soon fell in with Brian Jones, which was by no means a bad move. Being seen around town with the chippy-ruffian Stones, absorbed by the same parties, feted and fawned-over at the same gilded events, was doing the giant drummer and manic-fingered Pete no harm whatsoever. It's never what you know, is it. The pair of them milked it to the brim, and who could blame them? They'd have been stupid not to. I would have done it myself. That the Stones rated the Cheynes was tantamount to endorsement.

The Cheynes' line-up changed over time, as line-ups always do. Roger Peacock came in on vocals, while Phil Sawyer, who was destined for Fleur de Lys and then the post-Winwood Spencer Davis Group, took over on guitar. Roger and Mick moved in together, into a miniscule flat in Bayswater. The harmonious set-up was soon shattered, however, when Roger started going out with Jenny Boyd:

the younger, prettier sister of George Harrison's girlfriend Pattie. The problem was that Mick had fallen passionately in love with Jenny, but had been too painfully shy to ask her out. Despite the obvious domestic challenges, Mick and Jenny became close friends. Jenny worked for Foale & Tuffin, two young, female Royal College of Art graduates who ran their own design studio off Carnaby Street. Mick started visiting her there, behind his singer's back. Did all that early dishonesty and covert carrying-on set the precedent for inter-band love rivalry that would beset Mick's future superstar band Fleetwood Mac in years to come, and provide the template for the backdrop of their most celebrated album *Rumours*? Isn't it tempting to suppose so. Meanwhile, Ray Davies and his band had gone stratospheric. Pop music was all about the Beatles, the Rolling Stones, the Animals and the Kinks. One of us! If he could do it, we could do it! There was everything to play for.

Life at home had become impossible. My gross misdemeanour had not been forgiven. Every opportunity that arose to remind me of it was taken, and used as an excuse to castigate me. I had humiliated them all, I had sullied the family's good name, I came home too late, I kept them awake at night, I had thrown away my education, I was wasting my life, I was too untidy, I didn't wash enough, my table manners had disintegrated, I had no respect, I kept the wrong company. Everything was wrong with me. Everything about my lifestyle jarred with their expectations of me.

I could see all too clearly that my relationship with my parents stood no chance of improving until I enforced some distance between us and pressed Pause for a while. So I left home. My bravado was all front. I was not nearly as courageous about it as I was making out. My parents did not take the news well, but nor did they try to stop me. There was no remonstration, no hysteria. I may have sweated a little over the decision, but neither blood nor tears were shed. Had I been expecting any? It's hard to say. I suppose I might have felt more loved and appreciated, if I'm honest, had Mum and Dad relented and tried to persuade me to remain. But neither of them did, and I was damned if I was going to beg. I stiffened my upper lip, tightened my grip on my suitcase handle and on the case of my bass guitar, and sauntered off down the road without a backward glance. Stuff them, I thought. I didn't say 'stuff'. I would make my own way, without resorting to sponging off my family. Did they regret letting me go? If they did, it was never discussed. Not within my earshot, at least. Nor did they ever call to say, 'Come home, all is forgiven.' I reassured myself that this was normal, that this was what being young, free and single was all about. Fleeing the nest and living life independently in the capital was the adult thing to do. As far as I was concerned, I was now a fully-fledged London boy. I would be unencumbered by the expectation and judgement of my Dad. I was free to what I wanted, when I wanted, and I was terrified.

★

At least I had a roof over my head. I'd managed to find some digs, a small, shared bedsit in a big old Victorian house on Phillimore Gardens within walking distance of home. My flatmate was Gwen, an ex-girlfriend of Pete's. The set-up left a lot to be desired. For a start, there was only one bed, which was taken. The only other furniture was a geriatric camp bed and a gas fire. We had a kettle, but that was your lot. Whether or not there was carpet, I couldn't tell you, as the floor was covered entirely in Gwen's discarded clothes.

The camp bed collapsed the first night I tried to sleep in it. It was Gwen who suggested that I climb in with her. This was asking for it, we both knew, and sure enough it soon happened. I'm not sure who was the more embarrassed of the two of us the next morning. We tried to pretend that nothing had happened, for Pete's sake more than anything. While I felt sure that his relationship with Gwen was over and done with, it still felt somewhat distasteful to be stirring the porridge. Then again, I couldn't waste too much time and energy worrying about that. I was more concerned with how I was going to get a wash. While there was a toilet down the landing, we were without either shower or bath. I'm not sure that would even be legal today, but it seemed the norm back then. A bedsit was a bedsit. You slept in it and you sat in it. There was nothing in the job description about washing facilities. I coped with this for a bit by simply ignoring it, until I obviously became overpoweringly pungent. Gwen told me in the end that I stank, and that I needed a good wash. I wasn't entirely sure why she didn't. Anyway, she pointed me in the direction of a place on Adam and Eve Mews. I was rather baffled, when I arrived, to find myself among a bunch of formally-attired old men. How was I to know that I'd gone for a bath in a brothel?

Needs must. If I needed to wash it didn't much matter where I did it, provided I achieved the desired result. In a similar vein, I was penniless, and needed to pay the rent, so it hardly mattered what kind of job I did to earn it. I got a gig at Cohen's Smoked Salmon deli down Kensington High Street, where I took to playing my guitar in the basement when the boss was out. But when he offered me a promotion to manager, I ran a mile. I was by no means ready for the slippery slope of a run-of-the-mill nine-to-five job that might deprive me of my music and my art forever. Now what?

Believe it or not, I was still attending art school, where my heart wasn't in the art and where I was hanging by a thread. I was still playing my bass, in and out of a number of semi-pro line-ups and combos that seemed to be going nowhere fast. Surrounded by fellow-musician friends who were getting ahead, I began to fear that I was doomed to failure. Cut loose from my family, forever anxious about where the next fiver was coming from, I admit that it irked me to see Mick, Pete and the Cheynes touring, playing Oxford Street's Marquee Club and supporting some of the top acts of the day, such as the Yardbirds, the Zombies and John Mayall's Bluesbreakers, and jamming with Sonny Boy Williamson. Mick was also forging a friendship with the Bluesbreakers' bass player, a tax office worker called John McVie. If only any of us could have known what those two were heading for.

Despite my paranoia that everything was going well for everyone except me, things weren't as great for the Cheynes as their enthusiastic following suggested. The record-buying public didn't get them, and their singles continued to stiff. It was baffling: they were giving it their all to the point of exhaustion, and their live audiences loved them. They even talked themselves into a feature film, *Mods & Rockers*, performing Beatles covers, but then got left on the cutting room floor. By January 1965 it was all over. They went their separate ways. Pete was snapped up immediately to replace keyboard player Jackie McCauley in Belfast group Them with a mad, moody frontman by the name of Van Morrison. Mick moved out of the Bayswater flat he'd been sharing with Roger Peacock, at about the same time that Roger split up with Jenny. At long last, Mick and Jenny got together. If ever a couple was made for each other, it was those two.

Mick responded to an ad in the *Melody Maker* from the Bo Street Runners, an R&B outfit from Harrow whose name was inspired by bluesman Bo Diddley, and joined them as their drummer. My best mates were sorted. I had nothing and no one. I didn't even have a bath to lie in.

9

THE ONE

I was lost in thought during a life-drawing class at the Byam Shaw one chilly afternoon when suddenly I became aware of a golden goddess. She appeared to be gazing at me as though I were the answer to all her prayers. It *was* me she was staring at, wasn't it? I glanced furtively around the studio, convinced that I must be mistaken and that she had eyes only for some other bloke. But no, her smoky peepers were focused full-beam on me. She looked quite smitten. Here we go again, I thought: the most beautiful girl I'd ever seen. She was a tall, slim, ice-cool blonde with chiselled cheekbones and quilted lips. Her appearance was exotic and mysterious. Posh totty meets fallen angel. Now what? I risked what I was convinced was my best seductive half-smile, which must have distorted itself into a gormless grin by the time it reached her. Or maybe it didn't, because she responded with a come-to-bed pout that not even Stevie Wonder could have mistaken. And we're off.

Any lascivious inclination I might have felt towards the generously-padded nude posed before me drained instantly from my loins. There was only one woman in the room, as far as I was concerned, and the flirty female of my new obsession was fully-clothed. Not that it taxed my imagination too greatly to perceive what delights lay beneath. I was slavering. I could barely wait for class to end so that I could get her on her own, whoever she was, and get to know her. Where do you start? Only everywhere. I was running before I could walk, I knew, but I was helpless to resist. During those first few moments, I think I dragged her entire life history out of the poor girl. Her name was Sue, how do you do. Sue Murray. Born in Bournemouth, moved with her family to India, was educated at a convent there, and had taken up painting after her parents relocated to Sri Lanka. When they returned to England and settled in London, she had applied and got in to the Byam Shaw. Why hadn't I set eyes on her before?

The long and short, I asked her out. She was The One, God help me, I couldn't conceal my desire. We convened for our date. I was as nervous as hell. I remember strolling down Kensington High Street with her on my arm that day, clocking the astonished looks on the faces of passers-by. They were all evidently in agreement with me that a creature of such intoxicating beauty couldn't possibly exist in real life, and that they must be dreaming. To give Sue her due, she seemed oblivious of the effect she had on others. This exquisite beauty was natural, normal and chatty, your typical girl next-door. I was the one who was in pieces. It pains me to report that I never did overcome my sense of complete and utter inadequacy in her presence. I wouldn't hear of her getting down off her pedestal. In the end my adoration proved too much. She got fed-up with me, who could blame her, and wound up chucking me unceremoniously in a café. She never looked back. Why would she? Sue got picked up, as we used to say in those days. She became a professional model, and was soon gracing the pages of *Vogue* and *Harper's Bazaar* alongside Twiggy and Jean Shrimpton. Like them she also made it in America. She even became the face of Yardley of London, back then a major cosmetic brand. She was soon a favourite of the big-name photographers, even of Richard Avedon, and a muse of enfant terrible David Bailey. The latter fell hook and line for her, and made her one of his 'Faces of '65'. He then ditched her for Catherine Deneuve, whom he married. Poor Sue saw the light, and right through the fakery of Swinging London. She fled back to India, where she meditated in the Himalayas, resumed painting, and eventually became a respected portrait artist in Boston. She had the last laugh. Women tend to.

Where was I, meanwhile? Still festering in bedsitland. I had graduated from Gwen's mattress only to go down in the world, room by room. Each successive place I rented was increasingly squalid. I took to staying out later and later to avoid whichever slum-like bolt-hole I was calling home at the time. I would return to my digs reluctantly, only to sleep. My mother would have collapsed, had she been aware of how I was living. What a state. My lifestyle could not be more at odds with Mick's and Pete's. They had gone up in the world, and were now sharing a swanky West Hampstead loft conversion with all mod-cons. They were playing host to an increasing circle of Beautiful People posing as friends, and held endless pot-smoking and record-listening parties. I did none of the smoking but more than my share of listening, desperately seeking clues as to how I too might land my big break. What were we playing? Bob Dylan, the Yardbirds, the Stones, the Who, the Kinks. Ravi Shankar, the guy who put the sitar in rock. The times they were a-changin' yet again, and the whole world except me seemed to be on drugs. But things moved rapidly in those days. Whatever was hip in '65 would be finished by '66. Keeping up with trends was a full-time job, if you could be arsed. If you cared about where it was at, you now knew to avoid the Ad Lib and make a beeline instead for the Scotch of St. James, the latest venue in which to see and be seen. Mick and Jenny relished the place, they were in their element there. But that shallow hipster scene was never for me. My inner fogey was catching up with and getting the better of me.

Was the regret of my estrangement from my family finally hitting home? It might have had something to do with it. I did miss them, it must be said, though no way was I crawling home with my tail between my legs. I was also still smarting from Sue having shown me the door. I focused inwards for a few months, and gave serious thought to how I should live my life going forward. It was time to get real. No more kidding myself that I was going to make it as a rock star. I invested all my time and energy in finding myself a regular office job. Perhaps there was something to be said for the humdrum nine-to-five existence after all. I was just getting into it and learning to accept my fate when, late in the autumn of 1965, I got a call out of the blue from Pete Bardens. He'd left Van Morrison and Them to throw in his lot with Mick Fleetwood, who had quit the Bo Street Runners and was now ready to do his own thing. They were launching a new instrumental band, Looners Ltd, in the style of Booker T. & the M.G.'s. Of all the useless rock'n'roll names…

Oh, and they needed a bass player… which underwhelmed me to the point that I had to cough myself out of yawning down the 'phone. Didn't Pete get it? I'd turned my back on rock'n'roll. I had turned over a new leaf. I had a nine-to-five job and a regular income. If I saved hard enough, I might soon have enough for a deposit on a house, or a flat at least, and could set about applying for a mortgage. I might even find myself a wife, a proper woman, not a clothes peg like Sue (I was still trying to convince myself that she wasn't The One) and have a few kids together. Despite what I perceived to be my parents' shortcomings, or maybe because of them, I wanted a family desperately. So I had to do the necessary in order to get one. No, I told Pete firmly, it was too late. I was over all that. I'd drawn a line. I'd have to be mad to fall for his starry-eyed schemes and dreams again. Besides, I'd already done my time in a Booker T. tribute act. No good could come of it. Next.

But he got to me. Which was so Pete. I couldn't stop thinking about him. How was I supposed to apply myself to my mundane new grown-up life and responsibilities when my mind was now whirring to the fantasy tune of being in a band again? What if Ray Davies, Mick Fleetwood, Pete Bardens, Brian Jones and all those other guys had become bloody great superstars in fifty years' time, and there would I be, just another flaky old has-been session guy, retired from an office job that had never brought me a minute's fulfilment, reduced to boring my grandchildren over and over with the sad fact that I'd once been one of them? That I'd been a contender? Yeah, right, go on then, Grandpa. Pull the other one.

I knew in a beat that I had no choice but to change my mind. It was a massive risk, and I would probably live to regret it. But reaching the end of my life in the awful knowledge that I'd been offered a second chance to follow my dream but had been too much of a big girl's blouse to take it was something I knew I'd regret more. I left it for a few hours, just to look cool, and then I called Pete back. Were they by any chance still in need of a bass player? Does the Pope shit in the woods?

10

THE GREEN GOD

The new band came together quickly. We were ready to start gigging within weeks. I hadn't realised how much I'd missed playing with Pete, and I'd forgotten what a really great drummer Mick was. It had also slipped my mind what a fucking prima donna Pete could be, but I supposed I could live with that. I loved the bastard.

As de facto head of the group, Pete took charge during rehearsals and steered the band in his direction, whether we wanted him to or not. Somebody had to, Mick didn't seem fussed, and I sure as hell wasn't up to it.

We had a buzzy R&B sound, dominated by Pete's Hammond organ-playing, that we told ourselves was unique. We had landed ourselves a management deal with Rik and Johnny Gunnell, a shrewd pair of right-geezer brothers with underworld connections and a background in prize fighting, street-market-running, jazz club-owning and all-round general up-to-no-good-ing, who presided over their bookings and management agency in an office on Gerrard Street. Also on their roster were Georgie Fame, John Mayall, Zoot Money, Long John Baldry and Chris Farlowe. The Gunnells booked the cream of visiting American acts, and wormed their own artists onto the bill as support. They were arch-hustlers. You didn't want to cross them, nor run into them by yourself down a backstreet on a dark night. People warned us we were risking our lives, signing up with such toe-rags. But they were toe-rags with a smile, who got results. We'd heard all about the way they threatened their artists if ever anyone tried to leave and take their chances elsewhere. The Gunnells were A-grade

Soho villains, we were in no doubt. Villains who would go on to join the Robert Stigwood Organisation later that decade, and take over that company's operations in Los Angeles and New York. They were going places, and we wanted to go with them. We took a chance. In for a penny. We were beggars, not choosers. We needed a break, and they were the ones most likely to get it for us.

One distinct advantage to placing ourselves under their wing was that the Gunnells owned their own club. They had come into possession, in 1959, of the fabled Flamingo on Wardour Street. Its reputation as a respectable jazz nightclub that had once welcomed Ella Fitzgerald, Billie Holiday and Sarah Vaughan to its former Coventry Street location had been batted aside to make way for its reincarnation as a celebrated Sixties den of iniquity. Prostitutes and pimps, gangsters and drug dealers cavorted there with American servicemen, musicians and jazz fans. The mood was cross-cultural and no-holds. By 1963 it had become a popular Mod hang-out, welcoming the usual – the Beatles, the Stones, the Who, Jimi Hendrix – alongside a host of emerging acts. Its jam sessions were legendary: complete unknowns jumping on stage alongside Stevie Wonder, Patti LaBelle, Jerry Lee Lewis and Bill Haley. Georgie Fame and his Blue Flames were the resident band. Otis Redding, Wilson Pickett, Eric Clapton, the Animals and Rod Stewart all came. As did Judy Garland and Muhammad Ali, when the latter was still fighting as Cassius Clay. Licensing laws were ignored, fights were frequent, and you took your life in your hands just to play there. We began our weekly residence, as Looners Limited, in September 1965.

They loved us. We changed our name more often than most people change their underpants, and still they loved us. Whether we were the Looners, the Pete Bardens Quartet, the Peter B's or Peter B's Looners, we were everybody's favourite opening act. Pete was now replicating the vocal parts of soul and R&B classics with mind-blowing turns on his Hammond organ, and thrusting himself deftly into the limelight. Our guitarist Mick Parker was miffed by this. He quit in protest. We waved him goodbye. Guitarists were ten a penny, and Pete soon found us a credible replacement, confusingly also called Pete. He didn't exactly blow us away at first, but I could see that there was something about him. Whatever it was, Pete Bardens had perceived it, and we just had to trust him that this guy was the one for us. The new guy looked a bit weird and wonderful, and would certainly prove to be a talking point, but I was yet to be convinced by his musicianship. I soon got what Pete Bardens saw in Peter Green.

Peter, who hailed from a poor Jewish family in London's East End, had been playing since he was eleven, purloining his brother Len's cheap Spanish guitar. He'd been in a number of bands before Pete found him, including Bobby Dennis and the Dominoes and the Muskrats. He'd contributed bass to the Tridents, the group from which the Yardbirds had poached Jeff Beck to replace Eric Clapton. He had also played briefly with the Bluesbreakers, standing in for Clapton when the latter absconded to spend the summer in Greece with a troupe of gypsy minstrels. Peter had then started pestering John Mayall for a break, at the Zodiac Club. It struck me as odd that he would do such a presumptuous thing. But Peter had not yet shown us his true colours.

He might have been Eric Clapton's biggest fan. He played a Gibson Les Paul because Eric did. He reproduced his riffs faithfully. If at first I was inclined to dismiss him as just another copycat, I would soon be eating my words. He grew on me. I enjoyed his company. We honed our act as the ultimate instrumental outfit. We found ourselves opening for Bo Diddley at The Flamingo. I started hanging with Peter socially. I confess to having been taken aback when we were sitting on the top deck of a bus one day and Peter interrupted himself mid-sentence to turn and stare deeply into my eyes. For a moment I feared he was going to confess undying love for me. What he actually said was, 'Dave, you've got the blues. And so have I.'

What was *that* supposed to mean? Was this some cack-handed way of telling me that he had written something new, and wanted to try it out on me? Could he be casting aspersions on my character, and telling me to my face what everyone else must be whispering behind my back: that I was a miserable sod and unbearable to be around? I was so taken aback that I could find nothing to say in response. I looked away and changed the subject, embarrassed and unnerved. He never said it again. I put his words right out of my mind. It was only much later that I would remember what he'd said that day, and would understand what Peter Green had been trying to tell me. I had *the blues*. I was a true musician. In my heart and in my soul, deep down. The syllables reverberated, articulating both salvation and condemnation. Peter recognised me because I was like him. As things turned out, in different ways, we were as doomed as each other.

★

1966 is recalled as the peak of the Swinging Sixties, when music, fashion and youth culture collided, establishing teenagers and young adults as demographics in their own right. It is revered by sports fans as the year when England's national football team won the FIFA World Cup for the first and only time, defeating West Germany 4-2. I wasn't ever much of a fan of football, and I have tended to recall that year for significant musical reasons.

January 1966 saw the Decca release of *Them Again*, the second album by Van Morrison's group Them, with Pete Bardens's mitts all over it. Particularly stunning was their cover of Bob Dylan's 'It's All Over Now, Baby Blue'. Its fantastic arrangement and haunting keys were our Pete personified. That the album failed to chart was of no consequence to us. When it peaked at 138 on the US Billboard charts, we couldn't have cared less. It was almost as though the making of real music was now *above* the endorsement of mere chart positions; that the discovery of the singular value of our coterie of superior musicians was only a matter of time. The charts *did* matter, of course, because they measured sales. Sales meant success equalled income. No getting away from that. Though we sometimes liked to kid ourselves that we were too highbrow for material considerations, not even we could live on thin air.

Now I knew for sure that I had done the right thing by sticking with Pete. He was working with the best, and he was going places. Wherever he led, I would willingly follow, convinced that my own upgrade to rock star was only a matter of time.

★

Rik Gunnell wasted no time in landing Peter B's Looners a record deal. Columbia took us on, and we were thrilled to bits. We were booked for a BBC radio session, Jazz Beat, to be recorded in February, and rehearsed a few numbers to decide our debut single. The main contender was a cover of Jimmy Soul's Calypso-esque 'If You Want to Be Happy', with its controversial theme about never making a pretty woman your wife. We were able to sidestep criticism for covering it thanks to the fact that Pete's Hammond organ replaced the vocal. The B-side would be a Bardens original, 'Jodrell Blues' inspired by the Cockney rhyming slang 'Jodrell Bank'. Boys will be boys. This moreish up-beat number featured Pete swaggering away on blues piano, which I secretly preferred to his organ-playing. Not that I was about to tell him that.

Peter Green had a searing, insistent guitar solo mid-way through 'Jodrell Blues' that sent shivers down my spine. It still does. I have never grown tired of listening to it. Watching him play, it was as though Peter and his instrument had become one; that the guitar had assumed his voice and that Peter himself was actually singing through it. It was extraordinary. I remember glancing at Mick in disbelief the first time Peter played it, and Mick staring back at me as if to say, 'Christ, where did *that* come from?' There was something almost spiritual about it, as if it had come from a higher plane. This was guitar-playing on a level that none of us had heard before. I remember thinking it made me feel exactly the way I'd felt that day on the top deck of a London bus, when Peter had spooked me with his mumbled few words about me having *the blues*. He clearly had a gift for cutting right to the meaning of things. His playing was so brilliant that he eclipsed Pete on keys. Shortly afterwards, we were performing one of our regular all-nighters at The Flamingo when Pete's organ expired mid-song. What happened next was truly astonishing. Without even a flicker of panic, Peter Green simply stepped forward and casually took over where Pete had left off, bridging the gap with inspired, sensational guitar-playing. It left the audience gasping. Yet again, Mick and I stared at each other. What wizardry was among us?

The recording session of our first single was overseen by Eddie Kramer, whose name would become synonymous with Led Zeppelin and Jimi Hendrix. The A-side cover went down well, but it was the B-side, 'Jodrell Blues', that demonstrated beyond doubt what a terrific band we'd become. The single came and went, which was par for the course. We were still having fun kidding ourselves that chart positions, sales and keeping our record company and management happy were of no consequence; the reason being that the record's failure to score us a hit did nothing to prevent the Gunnells getting us gigs. We 'did our ten thousand hours', getting tighter and tighter, and gaining better and more lucrative engagements. One such was at the celebrated Klooks Kleek Club upstairs at West Hampstead's Railway Hotel. We also played the Gunnells' new Ram Jam Club on Brixton High Road, which they'd named after Geno Washington's band. We supported Geno there. We opened for Little Stevie Wonder, Wilson Pickett and other 'names'. As thrilling as it was to share a bill with the stars, we derived infinitely greater pleasure from playing alongside the best of British, such as our stablemates Zoot Money's Big Roll Band, featuring future Police man Andy Summers. Our Peter Green got up and jammed with them one night. Mick and I looked on yet again in complete amazement, knowing that what we were witnessing had never been seen before. He had at last emerged from his dusty chrysalis to reveal himself as the rarest of specimens: a guitarist with a unique tone. This was a fantasy, and something that is impossible to achieve in the real world. And yet, there Peter was, making magic before our very eyes. It was like watching him *turn into* a Les Paul. It's the only way I can describe it. Convulsive, vibrato-heavy and groaning with emotion, with true blues, it was a sound from another world. What beneficent muse had descended? I thought back to the sideburned, bad-shirted Peter Green who had underwhelmed me with both his presence and his playing when he'd first appeared on the scene. Was it physically possible to improve this much, this fast, to the point at which you had completely reinvented yourself? I doubted it, and yet was confounded by the point-blank proof. Unless my eyes and my ears were deceiving me, which couldn't be the case because Mick Fleetwood was seeing and hearing all this too, this was precisely what Peter had done. People say, when we hit our stride at something, that 'all our pennies drop'. In Peter's case, someone or something had dropped about ten million pounds.

There was, as ever, a price to pay. That price was the dark side. The deep dysfunction in Peter's background that had driven him to such musical virtuosity had also made him weird and insecure. He was, for example, wracked by envy and despair. Although he played easily as well as his hero Clapton, in my humble opinion, the thing about Eric was that he also sang. Peter didn't. Couldn't? Who knew? Inferiority consumed him. He bemoaned the fact that he had such long way to go.

And then there was me. A mere also-ran. I might 'have the blues', according to Mr. Green, but I was by no means in the two Peters' hallowed league. Would I ever be? I could hardly imagine it. Still, I was a genuine paid-up Looner. I was playing bass in a proper band with some of the best musicians in London – perhaps even in the entire world. We were making records, getting gigs, covering the rent and experiencing life at a level most bedroom guitarists could only imagine. I was daring to dream of a future with... what? Hits in the charts? Money in the bank? My own roof over my head? A beautiful wife in my bed and a couple of kids running in the yard?

About that. I hadn't had a girlfriend for months. Still smarting from Sue Murray's callous dismissal of me, I'd lost confidence and had been keeping a low profile. My celibate misery must have started to show, because a few of my female friends started taking it upon themselves to try match-making me with their mates. Once chum, Sandra Lawrence, insisted that I meet her friend Sue. Wasn't I through with Sues? I felt queasily superstitious, or maybe I was trying to put myself off. Anything for an easy life, I thought, but Sandra wasn't having it. In the end I did allow her to set something up with the latest Sue. We fixed a date in a local pub. I rocked up at the appointed hour, to be confronted by a living doll.

Was this Elizabeth Taylor that I saw before me? Not quite, but she wasn't far off. Sue Rollins was a perfectly-poised, raven-haired beauty with a Baccarat crystal accent and a habit of calling everyone 'Daarhling'. Our first encounter was like an audition. She wasted no time in wowing me with how connected she was, how well-travelled, what a fixture she was on the Kensington/Knightsbridge scene. I'm not sure I got the chance, that first date, to even tell her that I was a musician. I barely got to let her know my name. Not because I was holding back: I couldn't get a word in edgeways. She didn't stop talking. She held court, her conversation more of a monologue peppered with famous names, outrageous occurrences and all manner of titillating gossip. I was transfixed by her glamour and chat. I sat gazing at her like a lovesick moron as she gassed away, enchanted by the sound of her own voice. She clearly loved an audience, and had found a willing spectator in me. I soon discovered where she got it from. Sue was a chip off the old block. Not just any old block: her father Len Rollins, a former Naval commander, was not only an hotelier but also the loud, dapper, convivial landlord of The Denmark on Old Brompton Road, one of South Kensington's most popular pubs. It was where all the Harrods shop girls used to congregate at the end of their working day. It also attracted the neighbourhood's many bright young flat-dwellers and bedsit tenants. The place would be so packed, some evenings, that the throng spilled onto the pavement and stood drinking in the street. A typical night out would kick off at The Denmark and proceed from party to party into the small hours. Come the late Seventies the place had become the meeting place of an altogether different clientele, not the kind who were out and about to pick up girls.

My parents knew of Len Rollins. In spite of themselves, they were impressed that I was courting his daughter. Had I managed to do something right, at last? Sue seemed quite taken with me, as far as I could tell. She was keen to introduce me to her mum and dad. Before long, I was invited to theirs for dinner at their home near Bognor Regis, West Sussex. I was all too eager for the encounter, having heard so much about them, especially her father. Sue was clearly a Daddy's girl. Unfortunately her Daddy didn't think a lot of me. I had barely taken my jacket off and sat down before Pa Rollins was throwing a wobbler, denouncing me rudely me as a 'gaunt, long-haired freak' with whom he had not the slightest inclination to share his dinner table. With that, he turned on his heel and stamped out, slamming the front door behind him, leaving the three of us – Sue, her mother and me – open-mouthed. While Mrs Rollins did her best to compensate for her husband's dreadful behaviour, and was admirably gracious towards me, Sue was inconsolable and sat sobbing into her wine glass. I should have shown more concern, I know, but I was somewhat preoccupied. Was I really that gaunt? Was my hair too long? As for 'freak': was I actually?

Needless to say, I was rather wary of Sue's two-faced father after that. He clearly couldn't be trusted. I'd sit observing him from a distance down at The Denmark. I'd eavesdrop on his slick patter, and watch the way he behaved towards his customers. He was respect and dignity personified. So which was the real Rollins: the jovial publican or the private ill-mannered curmudgeon? I was reminded of Noël Coward's observation, in his play *Design for Living* of some thirty years earlier, that we all wear masks to protect ourselves from modern life. Perhaps Sue's father secretly hated his job, and deployed the affable alter ego as a survival device. As time ticked on, it occurred to me further that Sue had probably lifted a leaf from his book and was doing the same. For all her seductive effervescence and compelling, chattering company, she was unfortunately prone to tantrum-throwing and sulking. She could be crushingly unkind. She had a lashing tongue. Her Jekyll and Hyde personality really worried me. Her apparent adoration of me, a dishevelled, long-haired musician who quite clearly wasn't good enough for her, not only baffled Len, but drove a wedge between father and daughter. His disdain for Sue's boyfriend had the knock-on effect of causing her to lose respect for me. She had been captivated to begin with by my bohemian rock'n'roll lifestyle and the eccentric people who inhabited my world. All too soon, she was treating my friends and me with nothing but contempt.

11

SHOTGUN EXPRESS

I avoided the issue of 'How do you solve a problem like Sue Rollins' by burying myself in my music. Things were still happening for Peter B's Looners. Down at the Klooks Kleek Club one night, we were joined onstage by an extra-special guest singer. Rod Stewart was fast making a name for himself on London's R&B circuit with his gravel-in-a-biscuit-tin voice. Although he like to big up his allegiance to Scotland, his 'homeland', he was the son of a Scottish builder and an English housewife and had been born a stone's throw from where I came into the world, in London's Highgate. He had attended the same Secondary Modern school, William Grimshaw's, as Ray Davies, and had been part of the Ray Davies Quartet. He considered a career as a professional footballer, at one point, but wasn't quite up to the rigours of training. He'd thought he would give art school a go, and signed up at Hornsey Art College, where Ray went. The discovery that he was colour-blind soon thwarted that. He became a beatnik, went on marches, joined a commune, dug graves, got a job in a funeral parlour and ran around after blondes. He'd never given up his dream of being a singer. He had been in a few bands, including the Hoochie Coochie Men. Together with Brian Auger (the organist on the Yardbirds' 'For Your Love'), towering Long John Baldry, and fellow vocalist Julie Driscoll, Rod had been in blue-eyed soul outfit Steampacket.

Things went so well that night in the Kleek that Rod joined our band full-time. We kissed our instrumental-only ambitions goodbye. We conceded that, in order to have hits, we needed a voice. Rod fitted the bill, and displayed star quality right from the start. He refused to hump gear, for example. Lugging guitars and amps was far beneath him. He declined to spend his own money when somebody else's would do. And he was obsessed with his own appearance, stiffening his hair with sugar water and preening whenever he passed a mirror.

We now expanded our vocal line-up to include Beryl Marsden, a glam Toxteth toughie with heart and a massive voice who had sung at The Cavern, fronted the band the Undertakers, performed in Hamburg, had opened for the Beatles in 1965 on their final UK tour, was a favourite of their manager Brian Epstein – when he failed to sign Beryl, he nabbed Priscilla White and invented Cilla Black instead – and who had already released a few solo singles. She had shared a flat with Mick's girlfriend Jenny Boyd, which was how we knew her.

We now had the unique voices of raspy Rod and breathy Beryl. We had the keyboard-playing brilliance of Pete Bardens, the dazzling drumming of Mick Fleetwood and the genius, other-worldly guitar-playing of Peter Green. We had me on bass. We needed a new identity, and soon settled on Shotgun Express. Having examined what the Mamas and the Papas were doing on the West Coast of America, we knew that we now had all the elements in place to relaunch ourselves as a major chart act. What could possibly go right?

Truth be told, there is room in any one band for only one demanding diva. In Pete Bardens, Rod and Beryl, we had three, with Mick and me bringing up the rear. Gigantic personalities and menacing musical talent do not a harmonious line-up tend to make. Peter Green, the quiet one with the greatest virtuosity, was growing increasingly horrified by all the drama. I could tell, long before he told us, that he couldn't take much more.

A new set of photographic portraits was now commissioned by the Gunnells to promote the band, featuring our stunningly gorgeous new singers with Pete Bardens. All three were clutching rifles and sported magnificently sculpted hairdos. Got up in great garb, they looked fantastic. Mick Fleetwood had dressed like a rock star for years. It was only Peter Green and I who were letting the side down. He could do the business effortlessly with merely a neck scarf, I noticed, while I was still lamentably scruffy, no matter how hard I tried. I was told by the others to smarten myself up. It was time to go shopping. What was it to be? Silk, velvet, chiffon? Stripes, checked, polka-dot? Finery was confounding, but I could hardly be blamed. I had other, more fundamental things on my mind.

Such as, Sue and I getting married. Which we did, off-the-cuff, all too impulsively. Despite my misgivings about her, perhaps a little too hastily, possibly thumbing our noses at her disapproving father. Yes, most likely because he didn't want us to. It was a fun little wedding, nothing posh. We held our reception in a diner and went home to a beautiful apartment with a little garden on Kensington's Ifield Road. The partying began.

Marry in haste, repent at leisure. No aphorism was ever more loaded. Passionate romance gave way to turbulent marriage. The sad fact was that Sue adored the reflected limelight, and loved the idea of being with a musician, but she hated the reality of it. Most evenings, I was away or late home. When I was there we did little but argue, with Sue finding fault with every little thing I did or didn't. A hitherto carefully-concealed violent streak soon reared its ugly head. On more than one occasion I found myself pitching up for a Shotgun Express photo shoot with scratches all down my face. She smashed my guitars, destroyed my paintings, and attacked me constantly. I was physically and mentally abused. She was angry that I hadn't bought her an Aston Martin and a mansion in the country. Her ever-present father seemed to loathe me more by the hour. How delighted he must have been that she and I were not getting on.

★

Anguish at home, trouble at t'mill. While Shotgun Express had everything going for it, for Peter Green it had become too much. The minute Eric Clapton quit the Bluesbreakers to launch his own band Cream with two former members of the Graham Bond Organisation, singing bassist Jack Bruce and crazed drummer Ginger Baker, Peter left us to take Eric's place in John Mayall's band. I was secretly relieved, though I would never have said so. The kind of music we were now making was edging further and further away from the pure blues in which Peter excelled. Which was his life blood, in fact. Our new single for Columbia, 'I Could Feel the Whole World Turn Round,' was frothy nonsense, a mad, awkward confection of orchestrated pop and bona fide blues. It was, frankly, offensive, and made a mockery of all our musicianship. We hadn't even written it ourselves. The song on which Rod and Beryl duetted so valiantly was the work of Ray Smith and Tony Colton, he whose Big Boss Band I'd once played in, and was designed to guarantee us the ever-elusive hit record. We were selling out, and compromising our integrity. No wonder Peter couldn't stand it anymore. Out he went and in came John Moorshead, all too soon to be replaced by former Cheynes guitarist Phil Sawyer. The great irony was that it didn't actually matter a toss who we had on guitar, as we didn't get to play on our own record. Ray and Tony got so pissed off with us messing about in the studio, turning up late, smuggling girlfriends in and getting off our heads on booze and drugs – doing all the things we thought rock stars were supposed to do – that they banned us, and got a bunch of session guys in instead. This was common practice in those days, if quite scandalous. There are endless infamous examples of artists who never played on their own recordings. To avoid being sued, I had better not go there. Our own record, infected with schmaltzy strings and completely unrepresentative of the way we performed live, confused our fans and didn't exactly inspire them to go out and buy it. We were about to celebrate another fantastic flop single. We released one last effort, 'Funny Coz Neither Would I' backed with Pete's 'Indian Thing', which none of us would later remember making and which even fewer fans bought.

The so-called greatest year in history, the year we were supposed to get our big break, was fast drawing to a close. We still hadn't had a hit. Peter Green was gone. Rod Stewart quit. Phil Sawyer dumped us for the Spencer Davis Group. Mick Fleetwood had his eye on a greater prize. For Shotgun Express, the bullets were spent, and the track was running out.

12

BECK AND CALL

I was still trying to figure out what on earth I was going to tell Sue when I got a call out of the blue from Rod Stewart. Did I fancy playing bass in Jeff Beck's new band? Does Dolly Parton sleep on her back?

Beyond the Yardbirds, the Wallington boy who'd made a guitar from a cigar box had come to see Shotgun Express live, and was blown away by Rod's vocals. They went off and got drunk at Jeff's Putney flat afterwards. The zip-fingered, beak-nosed rocker lured Rod into his new group, and Rod brought me. About which Beck didn't seem too excited. I remember the first time we conversed, my voice regressing to posh public schoolboy because I was so nervous at meeting him, he screwed up his nose, jabbed his finger in my face and scoffed, 'What the fuck is *that*?'

'*That*', aka yours truly, was obviously not rough and ready enough for Beck's liking. Rock'n'rollers weren't supposed to be middle-class chinless wonders. Rough diamonds, gritty East End-ers, estuary urchins and blunt northerners all fitted the bill, but toffs need not apply. The daft thing is, I wasn't a toff. Not strictly speaking. But Beck heard what he heard, and he didn't go a bundle. Which confused me, as Simon Napier-Bell, the sharp music business supremo behind the Yardbirds and a man as cultured and well-spoken as any you might care to name, still managed him, even though future Led Zeppelin honcho Peter Grant and pop Svengali Mickie Most were sniffing around. The former wrestler turned rock'n'roll chauffeur and bouncer and the former singing waiter had become manager and manager-producer respectively. They shared an office. They wanted Jeff Beck.

The sweet and sour smell of success was all over him.

It was Mickie Most who convinced Jeff that he had what it took to be a pop star. Beck sold out both himself and his band massively for a moment, when he agreed to record the catchy song 'Hi Ho Silver Lining' by American songwriters Scott English and Larry Weiss. The song would become Beck's trademark, a legacy he would later denounce as like 'having a pink toilet seat hung around my neck.'

Producer Most insisted that Jeff sang the lead vocal instead of Rod. Jeff agreed under sufferance, and Rod sang backing vocals. Jeff threw in a magnificently raucous guitar solo, and I played bass on it. So those who were there insist. I can't actually remember having done so, and the history books record the bassist as having been John Paul Jones. Who knows? They say that if you can remember the Sixties, you weren't there. I know I was there, and I do remember most of it, so I take issue with the axiom in this case. Whatever the truth, I never got paid for it.

The end result was football-terrace anthem meets office booze-up famously described as 'psychedelia for the suburbs'. It captured the public's imagination, and was a March 1967 Top Twenty hit. Its B-side, 'Beck's Bolero', had been recorded the previous year while Jeff was still in the Yardbirds. Having had it up to here with Pete Townshend's control freakery, the Who's drummer Keith Moon and their bassist John Entwistle agreed to do some experimental recording with Beck and axeman Jimmy Page, along with celebrated session pianist Nicky Hopkins. But Entwistle lost his nerve at the last minute, fearing the wrath of Townshend, and withdrew. John Paul Jones stepped in. 'Beck's Bolero', Jeff's rock variation on Ravel's classical original and sexed-up with an insistent new melody, arose out of those law-breaking sessions. This amazing track, complete with Keith screaming in the middle over the drum break – after which you could hear only the cymbal because Moonie knocked the mic over – could not have been further-removed in style from the happy-go-lucky 'Silver Lining'. It was so much more 'Jeff', and infinitely more faithful to his roguish, volatile, unpredictable musical integrity. It was indicative of what Beck's new line-up would be capable of achieving over the gigs, singles and albums to come.

But the Jeff Beck Group let themselves down with a disastrous debut in support of the Small Faces at London's Finsbury Park Astoria (the future Rainbow) that March. A string of timely technical mishaps did little to disguise the fact that the band was under-rehearsed. With Rod Stewart on lead vocals, Jeff on lead guitar and Ronnie Wood on the bass – Rod and Ronnie were so similar in appearance, personality and sense of humour that they could have been brothers, a fact which delighted their audience – there was really no excuse for that shoddy performance.

It should have been me, not Ronnie, on bass. I had actually been the official bassist for a while. But Beck never took to this hapless, sneering toff, so I was never going to stay the course. Neither did the Shadow nor the Pretty Thing they trialled. Nor did a single one of their try-out drummers. The endless personnel changes, a complicated management structure and an identity crisis made blatantly apparent by the contradictory clash of their first single's two sides, cast doubt on the Jeff Beck Group's ability to survive. Did Beck want to be a cutesy pop idol or a worthy rock guitar hero? Which audience was he chasing? He had to choose one or the other, but he didn't seem capable of making up his mind.

Jeff did warm to me in the end. In his own way, at least. Sue and I took him down the pub and under our wing on several occasions, whenever he got depressed. At one point I went round to his flat in Sutton with a bunch of my own precious blues records under my arm, to cheer him up. It was vinyl that I would never set eyes on again. Shortly after that visit I was fired from the Jeff Beck Group. Ronnie Wood was back on bass. Thinking back over the roll call of superlative musicians who had found themselves consigned to the wheelie bin of Beck's endless re-evaluation, I could hardly feel bad about it.

But here I was again, fresh out of a job.

Since he was the one who had talked me into joining Jeff Beck in the first place, Rod must have been feeling guilty about my sacking. I got a call from him less than a week after I was shown the door, to say that he'd got me onto a somewhat eccentric package tour. It featured the Walker Brothers, Engelbert Humperdinck and Cat Stevens, whose backing band had Jimi Hendrix on bass. I laughed out loud when Rod read me the line-up. I was hardly in any position to refuse.

I was a big fan of Cat Stevens's songwriting. When I joined his band on that strangest of bills, one of Jeff Beck's exes, the superb Mickey Waller, was on drums, and the guitarist was the exceptional session man Ray Russell. The brass section featured Roger Thornton and Barry Noble. As delightful to work with as Cat was, his producer/manager Mike Hurst made it difficult for us to enjoy working for him. The remuneration was piss-poor, certainly not enough to cover board and lodging on the road, which we often had to pay for ourselves. Exasperation got the better of us one night, when we decided to steal all Cat's clothes just before he was due on stage. No, it wasn't fair to take it out on him, but desperate times call for desperate measures. He was forced to appear dressed in nothing but his overcoat. At least we left him that. He probably had no idea that his management was ill-treating his band, and paying us way less than we were worth. But there must have been other issues that were not to Cat's liking. Soon after that surreal tour concluded, he and his management went their separate ways.

While we had been amusing ourselves stealing the star's wardrobe, Jimi Hendrix had been busy stealing the show. The headlining Walker Brothers in particular took exception to the way this down-bill upstart fellow American was flooring audiences with his frenzied guitar-playing. With Noel Redding on bass and Mitch Mitchell on drums, his Jimi Hendrix Experience was killing the competition. But it wasn't just about musicianship. Behind the scenes, unbeknown to the other musicians, the band's manager, former Animals bassist Chas Chandler, rock writer Keith Altham and Jimi had conspired to come up with a headline-grabbing gimmick that would take Jimi to incendiary heights.

Backstage at the Finsbury Park Astoria on 31st March, the night of the tour's first show, the trio sat discussing a new song the Experience had started performing, called 'Fire'. Wouldn't it be cool, Keith said, if Jim played 'Fire' and then played with fire for real. Chandler and Jimi leapt at it. A roadie was dispatched to purchase some lighter fuel. On stage, at the appropriate moment, having just delivered the number, Jimi set down his Fender Stratocaster next to the amp then moved to the front of the stage to distract the audience while Mitch and Noel kept jamming away and Chandler crept on to drench the instrument in the lighter fuel. Jimi then returned to his guitar, fell to his knees and struck a few matches, and eventually managed to set it alight. He got more than any of them had bargained for. Chandler had poured so much lighter fuel that the flames leapt higher than Hendrix himself.

He was not the only one who sustained injury. The shocked compere of the show rushed forward to tackle the blaze with a fire extinguisher, and was burned. Hendrix, unfazed, performed his grand finale on a replacement guitar before they were both carted off to the local hospital for treatment. The dangerous stunt was a one-off. Not that they needed to do it again. Headlines had been grabbed. Hendrix's name was made. Although Jimi did give it another go for posterity during his unforgettable performance at the International Pop Music Festival in Monterey, California, three months later, stealing the show yet again: this time from Otis Redding, Janis Joplin, Ravi Shankar and the Who. It wasn't until 2008, having languished for more than forty years in storage, that the blackened Strat from that fateful Finsbury Park night cooked up by the fabled Keith Altham was extracted from storage and sold at auction for nearly £400,000.

As we were packing our bags and preparing to depart on that strangest of tours, Jimi's second single 'Purple Haze' was on the verge of being released in the UK. The first time I heard it I wondered what the hell had hit me. Its psychedelic sound aroused all the senses. It was a mass of contradictions: discordant and melodic, sinister and sensuous, explosive and mellow. It was both in your face and far, far out. It wasn't the first time that a distinctive guitar riff had upstaged a vocal – think the Kinks' 'You Really Got Me', the Stones' 'Satisfaction' or the Yardbirds' 'Heart Full Of Soul' (the 'birds' distinctive singer Keith Relf was electrocuted to death nine years later, while playing his guitar in his basement.) Because its riff eclipsed every other aspect of the record, 'Purple Haze' was in a class of its own. I didn't become friends with Jimi on the tour, but I got to know what he was like from what others said about him. They all said the same thing: that he was a sweetheart, a gentleman, and nothing like the deranged performer who hollered his lyrics with an orgasmic abandon that almost made Jagger seem demure. When I came to read about Jimi's childhood and upbringing following his death three years later at the age of twenty-seven, I learned exactly where all that music had come from. Dysfunction, distortion, abandonment and abuse and were the name of the game, as they have been for so many exceptional artists.

★

I hadn't been home long after the tour concluded when Sue and I were called upon one night by two unexpected visitors: Mick Fleetwood and Peter Green. Mick had recently replaced Aynsley Dunbar in John Mayall's Bluesbreakers, but his tenure had lasted only a month and a half. Their bassist John McVie and Mick had become deadly drinking partners. An incident on tour in Ireland had been enough for Mayall to kick Mick out and to replace him with Keith Hartley. Peter Green soon followed Mick, of his own accord, explaining that the chemistry wasn't there without Fleetwood. As a parting shot of goodwill, John gifted Mick, Peter and John McVie some studio time at Decca in West Hampstead. They had emerged with a number of tracks of worth, the most distinctive of which was a twelve-bar Chicago blues piece onto which Peter had overdubbed a miraculous whimpering harmonica part. They had called it 'Fleetwood Mac'. The name crystallised in my head the moment I heard it.

Peter Green's guitar-playing was better than ever. Check out his 'The Supernatural' on the Bluesbreakers' early 1967 album *A Hard Road* if you don't believe me. The penetrating piece is a masterclass in atmospheric guitar-playing that set a precedent for further brilliance to come. I am talking, of course, of his magnum opus 'Albatross', and of the album *Then Play On*. Peter's sensitive and original interpretation of the blues, like Hendrix's, rendered other attempts staid and routine. He wasn't Clapton, nor was he Beck. Peter was in a class of his own, the realisation of which must have absolutely terrified him. Not only that, but those around him, all too aware of his brilliance, now wanted to exploit him and make him a star. The rottweilers were throwing themselves in his face. Clifford Davis, a booker at the Gunnell agency, tried to make Peter go solo so that he could manage him. Mike Vernon, a staff producer at Decca Studios who had overseen the Bluesbreakers' sessions, sought to sign Green's latest project to his independent blues label Blue Horizon. All that Peter wanted to do was play his guitar.

Was it ever that simple? Who knows. Because of the way that Peter Green's sad story unfolded down the years, a litany of schizophrenia and drug abuse, we were all seduced by the notion of a puzzling individual who perhaps never truly existed. The self-effacing musician burdened by unbearable talent that he resisted exploiting for money or fame was for all the reasons irresistible. But it wasn't quite like that.

Most of the best artists I've encountered or worked with have one thing in common: they are the ultimate contradiction of extreme self-belief and crippling self-doubt. Peter was like that. The paradox lent majesty to his musicianship. That majesty was overshadowed by human weakness, condemning him to a life of bleak despair.

13

MAKING IT

When Peter Green and Mick Fleetwood decided to launch a new group, it wasn't clear what kind of set-up they had in mind. They had already failed in their attempt to lure John McVie away from John Mayall. For now, at least. Not only had he had a steady gig with Mayall for five years, but by all accounts he wasn't keen on the manager of the new group, Clifford Davis. They had then approached Ric Grech of Family, who would go on to star in supergroups Blind Faith and Traffic, but he was staying put too. So I was their third-choice bassist, which is what Peter and Mick came round to my flat to tell me. Some might have taken that as an insult. But I couldn't do that, as they presented it to me as a great privilege. Their enthusiasm was so touching that it moved me. They also announced that they had decided on a name for the band: the very name of that haunting instrumental 'Fleetwood Mac'. It must have seemed odd to me at the time that they had decided to incorporate the nickname of a musician who wasn't even in the band, but I kept schtum about it. It has long been rumoured that Peter Green coined their moniker, so confident was he that John 'Mac' McVie would come running if they named the group in his honour. Apart from Clifford Davis having agreed to manage them and Mike Vernon having offered them a contract with his label Blue Horizon, nothing else was set in stone. It never really would be. This was to set the precedent for the eccentric manner in which Fleetwood Mac conducted themselves for decades to come.

What do you think I said? You *bet* I jumped at it. How great was this, to be back doing what I did best, in the company of my favourite old Shotgun Express band mates?

Everyone was delighted that I had joined Fleetwood Mac. Everyone, that is, except Sue. She couldn't stand the idea of me hanging out with Mick again. He was bound to corrupt me, she wailed. He'd go leading me astray. He'd have me in rehearsals, on the road and in and out of seedy clubs all the time, she moaned on, and what about the *fucking bills*? Because the last thing I'd be doing in Fleetwood Mac would be making any money. What about my responsibilities to our marriage? She also spat at me for good measure that Shotgun Express hadn't exactly set the charts alight, had they. She went on and on until she dragged me down, until it was more than my life was worth. I was that beaten by her, I didn't know how to tell the guys. I simply stopped turning up to rehearsals. I had to tell them eventually, but only when they came looking for me and asked me to my face. I was devastated. This was everything I'd ever wanted. These superlative musicians had put their faith in me, and I had let them down. I knew as I was articulating my grovelling apology to them that I would never in my life get such an opportunity again.

What choice did they have but to seek another bass player? A Wanted ad in the *Melody Maker* somehow featured the wrong 'phone number, despite which Five's Company bassist Bob Brunning managed to get in touch and secure himself the position that was rightfully mine. Peter subsequently decided that he would feel more confident when performing if he could share the stage with a second guitarist. Mike Vernon found them Jeremy Spencer, a Staffordshire art college graduate with a penchant for Elmore James. The band were now billed as Peter Green's Fleetwood Mac. The wizard guitarist's name was featured to ensure fans knew that the famous former Bluesbreaker was part of the line-up. Typically of Peter and his withdrawn personality, he would insist on the deletion of his name as soon as the new group had established themselves. This was perhaps a premonition of his eventual departure.

They made their debut at the Windsor Jazz and Blues festival on a Sunday night during August 1967, in ironic support of the Bluesbreakers, who now had Mick Taylor on guitar, he who would proceed to replace Brian Jones in the Rolling Stones. John McVie caught their performance before he took to the stage with the Bluesbreakers. Come Christmas, he would have taken his rightful place in the band that already bore his name.

Was I snivelling around at home, slashing my wrists and gnashing and wailing that it should have been me? Not exactly. Before the new Fleetwood Mac had even played their first gig, I had signed up to another band that was going to take me further than they ever could. Right? This genre-blurring outfit, fronted by gifted organist Brian Auger and magnetic vocalist Julie Driscoll, were so full of promise that I would never again need to look beyond the Trinity.

★

Brian Auger's is a name that few remember today. There was a time when mere mention caused a frisson in inner circles. He was a serious musician, and suffered no fools. His was that fine filigree of harpsichord-playing on the intro of the Yardbirds' 'For Your Love'. He had even been crowned 'Best New Hope of 1964' by the *Melody Maker's* jazz fans three years earlier. The Trinity had made a name for themselves with their powerful blend of R&B and jazz infused with diverse musical condiments to spice the effect. Julie Driscoll, the singer, was a beauty with bursting lungs. She had 'Star!' written all over her. I was nervous when I went along to meet them, despite having played with Brian before: on an air force base, filling in at the last minute. At the end of the gig, he had smiled, and had shaken my hand. It had felt like an endorsement.

En route to our first official meeting, I searched my memory for anything that Rod Stewart might have told me about Brian from the days when they played together in Steampacket. Was self-taught virtuoso Auger, as was rumoured, really a mad musical despot and relentless taskmaster who would make my life a misery – in the unlikely event that he would hire me? I could remember the Trinity's ever-shifting line-up playing the circuit – Ronnie Scott's, The Marquee and The Flamingo – in parallel with the Looners. The crowd at The Flamingo in particular loved them, as did our manager Rik Gunnell. The Trinity's blend of funky rhythms and sophisticated jazz was right up his street. When Georgie Fame was unable to perform because a day at the beach had left him lobster-red and writhing in pain, Rik got the Trinity to fill in for him and the Flames. It was Rik who urged Brian to switch from piano to Hammond organ, which he took to like a mallard to a moat.

He could play the organ the way Eric Clapton, Jeff Beck and Peter Green played their guitars. The Trinity had released a few records, but nothing chart-worthy. Brian's name began to reverberate following his guest appearance with the Yardbirds, orchestrated by their shared manager Giorgio Gomelsky. Long John Baldry caught up with Brian playing at Manchester's Twisted Wheel, and suggested that they go in together. Brian agreed to it, and Baldry would disband his Hoochie Coochie Men to create a new one with the Trinity as backing band. He added that there was just one more thing. He threw in his protégé Rod Stewart. They later decided to add a female voice, just as we had in Shotgun Express with Beryl Marsden. The girl they chose was the secretary of the Yardbirds' fan club, one Julie Driscoll from South London.

Steampacket were a massive success with live audiences. Both the Beatles and the Stones were said to love them. But they suffered the same fate as Shotgun Express, in that live-performance popularity failed to translate into record sales. Not that they could record as a single unit, because they were all signed to different labels. Julie Driscoll was represented by Parlophone, Rod Stewart by Columbia and Long John Baldry by United Artists. It was all too complicated. An ill-fated residency in St. Tropez was the catalyst for their demise. Rod came to us in Shotgun Express. Baldry started drinking himself stupid. Brian stepped away from the touch paper, and retreated to revive the Trinity. Julie Driscoll came back. Now here we all were.

My mind was brimming with so much history, music and facts by the time I arrived that I could barely remember the reason I was there. I needn't have worried. Brian turned out to be a cool dude. He was friendliness and enthusiasm personified. He didn't stand to attention, and had a great sense of humour. He larked about impersonating Germans and reproducing Goons sketches. He was clearly passionate about his music, but wasn't at all the jazz snob some cracked him up to be. I liked him. He seemed to like me too. I was invited shortly afterwards for an audition at Blaise's, a cramped little basement venue beneath the Imperial Hotel on South Kensington's Queen's Gate, where Hendrix and Pink Floyd had played. Things went well. I got the job. Sue would be delighted, and I would be off the hook. I breathed a sigh of relief. Not only was this guaranteed income but it was an opportunity to raise my game. I was a good musician, Brian said. He was going to make me a great one.

★

It soon became apparent that one of Brian's great strengths was loyalty. He remained faithful to his band mates in the face of temptation too great for most musicians to resist.

Having been one of the first British musicians to play with Jimi Hendrix when the American arrived in London, co-managers Chas Chandler and Michael 'Mickey' Jeffrey decided that Jimi should join the Trinity. When Chas asked Brian to audition Jimi, Brian recoiled. Knowing Jeffrey to be the kind of villain he had always gone the distance to avoid, Brian made his excuses and declined. The thing was, he already had Vic Briggs on guitar.

Brian was, however, amenable to Jimi joining the group for a jam, down at the Cromwellian. In the basement of the club where Rod Stewart had first met Jeff Beck, Auger played alongside the future legend Hendrix. The latter enquired of the former as to whether he knew the chords to 'Hey Joe', and away they went. The audience was transfixed. A few months later, I appeared on the same bill as Jimi when I was playing with Cat Stevens's band. I now found myself in the group that Jimi had jammed with. Vic Briggs had retreated to join Eric Burdon's new psychedelic Animals, and Gary Boyle, formerly of Dusty Springfield's band, had replaced him. Round and round we went.

The Trinity I joined during the Summer of Love were a motley crew. I liked all the musicians in the line-up, especially our singer. I tried my damnedest not to like her too much. I pulled muscles trying to avoid being star-struck on stage with Julie, and focused pointedly on my bass parts rather than on *her* parts. Which was no mean feat. Julie was Tinkerbell: elfin-faced, smudgy-eyed and chalky-lipped, with short, sharp hair and a fierce stage presence. She sang like the seasoned diva she was, having worked the London clubs with her father from an early age. She was unpredictable, bewitching, other-worldy. When I first saw Robert Plant perform a few years later, so much about him reminded me of Julie. What a versatile vocalist she was. She had released her own singles, featuring Brian, and continued to record as a solo artist while performing in the group. Her single 'I Know You Love Me Not' was the one that really got me. It was more Dusty than Dusty. Everyone fell for her. I was intoxicated in her presence, which must have shown, because she was cool towards me to begin with. The ice thawed after a while, however. She relaxed in my company and came to treat me as one of the boys and not a gormless, lust-struck dope.

Not long after I joined the band, Brian called me with a list of songs he wanted me to learn. Before I had worked my way through it, he turned up at my place early one morning in his blue VW Beetle and told me to throw a few things in a bag and hop in, we were going to the South of France. I left Sue standing on the doorstep, open-mouthed. Looking back, I can see all too well that I was falling somewhat short in the spouse department.

We drove non-stop to Milan, then on to St. Tropez. We had a sandwich somewhere en route, but zero sleep. After grabbing four hours' kip on arrival, it was straight on stage at the Voom Voom Club, where Brian had managed to land us a fortnight's residency. Those shows felt like extended auditions. We played three-and-a-half-hour sets that had our eyes out on stalks and which pushed us to our musical limits. In spite of which, I adored it. I was doing my 'ten thousand hours' and getting a holiday at the same time. I shopped for cool clothes, bronzed myself on the beaches among the barely-clad beautiful people, and started kidding myself that I'd made it.

But all good things come to an end. Back in the UK we gigged ourselves stupid, from the Cromwellian to the Bag O' Nails, a favourite haunt of Paul McCartney's. We played Pink Floyd's psychedelic International Love-In at the Alexandra Palace, alongside the New Animals, Tomorrow and the Crazy World of Arthur Brown. Life was good, if hectic, and the pay cheques came on time. I was covering the rent and the bills, which was a huge relief. This went a long way towards promoting domestic harmony. I'd even managed to buy myself an MGB. I didn't have it long before I almost wrote it off. I walked away virtually unscathed from the accident, but Sue was furious, as a period of penury ensued. I half-starved us in order to save enough to repair the car, by which she was not amused. I still miss that motor. I wonder where it is now.

The time came for the Trinity to record our first LP. Entitled *Open*, it featured both original material and covers, most of them selected from our gigging repertoire. Recording at Chappell Studios was completed in no time, just a couple of days. This despite the fact that we had an in-studio audience for some of the sessions, our friends and family clapping along in the background. Those were happy moments, which lent a special magic to what we were laying down on tape. The recordings were divided into two distinct sides, the first dedicated to 'Auge', the second credited to 'Jools', aka Julie. Brian did sing a number, the rather frantic 'Black Cat', but side one was predominantly instrumental. It was a showcase for what a powerhouse we had become. The Hammond-led 'Mod' grooves for which Brian had become famous soared throughout, especially on the opener: a cover of Wes Montgomery's 'In and Out'. On 'Lament for Miss Baker', an original, Brian demonstrated his Midas touch on the piano, skipping effortlessly between languid jazz and Erik Satie-style elegance. 'Goodbye Jungle Telegraph' was an exotic blend of afro-beat and voodoo bebop. On 'A Kind Of Love-in', a Trinity original on Julie's side, horns and organ blared an urgent Morse code-style stutter, a soulful nod to the Supremes' 'You Keep Me Hanging On', as a breathless Jools preached the hippy gospel of peace, love and unity. Also on Jools's side, we had 'Break It Up': another original and the only track I didn't play on. The remainder of hers were covers she'd selected herself, such as the Staples Singers' 'Why (Am I Treated So Bad)' and her scorching take on Lowell Fulson's 'Tramp'. Both were live favourites. On record, she smashed it. We all did. Blues, soul, jazz and psychedelia were all stirred into the Trinity cauldron. It was the kind of sound, blend and approach that came to be known as 'fusion'.

★

What do I remember of that long, hot Summer of Love? I remember the music that summed up the Sixties. Jimi Hendrix's *Are You Experienced?*, the Beatles' *Sgt. Pepper*, Pink Floyd's exquisite debut, *The Piper at the Gates of Dawn*. What promise had been captured in that clutch of classics-to-be. If we could have known then what we know now. If they could do it, we could do it. There was everything to play for. What blissful, barely imaginable brilliance the future now held.

14

THIS WHEEL'S ON FIRE

Everything had come together. All too soon, it would all start falling apart.

Not long after we finished recording the album, guitarist Gary Boyle left us for the Leeds School of Music. We didn't replace him. Our debut LP managed to miss its release date by a month, thanks to the fact that our management were focused on other projects, and much of our scheduled promotion had to be binned. We weren't happy about it, but didn't have time to care. We had gone through the roof in France, where our souped-up cover of Aretha Franklin's 'Save Me' was tearing up the charts, hitting the jackpot over New Year 1968. We were all over French TV. Julie was the quintessential soul-queen acid diva. They couldn't get enough of her.

Which was partly the problem. The album artwork was all Julie, with a throwaway shot of Brian on the back. Weren't we supposed to be a group? Our incendiary brass section weren't even credited. As offended as the rest of us were, this was nothing to what they did with the French release of 'Save Me'. Not only was Julie the only one of us featured on the sleeve, she was the only one whose name appeared too. Brian went nuts. He and our manager Giorgio fell out so badly over it that the rift would never heal. Brian now knew for certain what he had suspected for some time: that our management were hell-bent on marketing Julie as the star and the rest of us as merely her backing band. This made a mockery of everything we stood for. It reached the point, during interviews, when reporters who couldn't get near Julie were asking Brian who he was and what he did. We all knew it wasn't

Julie's fault. She was virtually devoid of ego, and was doing nothing to drive this campaign. It didn't come between her and Brian, incredibly. We all knew enough to realise that this was Gomelsky's doing, that he was cashing in on his star artist and wrecking the group in the process. Which is what happened to the Trinity. We disintegrated before we reached our true potential, and we didn't have ourselves to blame. Brian would later insist that we were 'over before we began.' It might have been wishful thinking. The irony was that the demise of the band eventually spelled the decline of Julie, too.

We soldiered on for a while, half-heartedly. Hendrix opened for us at the Paris Olympia. A year on, we'd be opening for him. We bagged a residency in glamorous Portofino on the Italian Riviera, in a castle overlooking the sea. The publicity was still Julie-Julie-Julie, which continued to irk Brian. Giorgio would shrug and say it was what the Italian promoters wanted. While Brian skulked around fuming at this state of affairs, I felt almost guilty that I got on so well with Giorgio. He was never less than pleasant to me, encouraging me to read more and keep up with my painting. A father figure? I suppose he was, in a way. It amazes me now to think that I was still only twenty-two.

For all the misery of everything else that was going on, touring Europe that year was fantastic. We played the best of the Italian radical discotheques emerging at the time, such as the Piper Club in Rome. The extreme lights and décor made you feel as though you were performing inside a giant art installation. We jammed with prog group Aphrodite's Child, featuring Demis Roussos and Vangelis. These were moments of respite from escalating tension. As was my philandering.

What was I supposed to say when a stunning Italian woman approached me after our residency in Portofino on the Ligurian coast, and asked me to accompany her back to Rome? Sue and I did nothing but argue. She kicked up such a fuss whenever I went on the road with the band that I dreaded returning home. What harm could there possibly be in a restorative fling? So, bastard unfaithful husband that I was, I threw caution to the wind and went. Things didn't quite work out as I'd expected. The moment we landed, the gorgeous woman who had seemed so enamoured of me promptly dumped me for a more handsome, wealthier man. Stranded in the Eternal City with barely a lira to my name, I was consumed with remorse. What good would that do? I justified it to myself with the thought that I had suspected for a while that Sue was being unfaithful too. It could only get worse.

★

At least the Trinity were about to get their last hurrah. Giorgio had procured a song from Bob Dylan's *Basement Tapes*, recorded with the Hawks (soon to be renamed the Band) during his lockdown in upstate New York after his July 1966 motorcycle accident. The song was 'This Wheel's on Fire', and he wanted the Trinity to record it. The lyrics were absurd, impenetrable, inscrutable, but the song had a nagging tune. There was something about it that seemed to sum up the end of the Sixties. Things were coming to a close, burning out around our ears. Disintegration was everywhere. The song that summed it all up would give us our biggest UK hit.

★

We performed at MIDEM in January 1968, the annual Cannes music business trade fair having been launched the previous year. Attracting thousands of musicians, producers, managers, lawyers, agents, record company executives and journalists, it was and is the beano at which to be seen. Performing alongside, among others, the Moody Blues, the Supremes, Nina Simone and Procol Harum, we went down a storm. Our cover of the Animals' 'Don't Let Me Be Misunderstood' knocked their eyes out. Some of them, anyway. Others clearly couldn't see the point of us, but I think we made an impression, at least. It was at MIDEM that the British press started to take notice of us. They wanted to know more about this home-grown act that was taking 'the Continent', as we used to call Europe, by storm with hits such as the hypnotic 'Season of the Witch' and a cover of Bob Dylan's 'I Am a Lonesome Hobo'. Who *were* we, and where had we come from?

Back home, we set about recording 'This Wheel's on Fire', and took our time over it. There was a tangible sense that this could be the breakthrough. We had one chance to get it right. Brian played piano, organ and mellotron: the strange keyboard, basically an early synthesiser loaded with tapes of pre-recorded sounds, which the Beatles used to sublime flute-like effect on 'Strawberry Fields' and which lent orchestral grandeur to 'Nights In White Satin' and other songs by the Moody Blues. It gave our track a mysterious edge. Julie's vocal was matchless, in another league, while the seductive and sinister walking bassline was all mine. The trippy song played out to the sound of Brian having a fight with his Hammond as if both were both literally on fire… if my memory serves me well.

The single was released that April, reflecting the mood of instability and unrest into which the Summer of Love had dissolved. Peace and love were out. The world was no longer idealistic. There were no longer flowers in our hair. Our record captured the zeitgeist, with which the record-buying public appeared to agree. We soared to Number Five on the national UK chart, and on the *NME*'s own chart we made it to the top. At last, our album *Open* started getting the attention it deserved, and became a Top Twenty hit, peaking at Number Twelve. We emerged blinking from the underground scene to find ourselves thrust into the limelight, onto every television show, into every newspaper and music rag. We were all over the radio. Fame at last.

Did this mean we were now pop stars? Among ourselves, we found the notion bizarre. But it didn't matter what *we* thought. Come June 1968, aficionados of *Top Of The Pops* sat down to be wowed by a brand-new star by the name of Julie Driscoll, oblivious of the fact that an entire band existed of which she was only a part. The cameras adored her, and so did the public. Could we really complain? We had achieved what we set out to. That Julie was the face of a group and not a solo artist with a few back-up musicians was of no consequence to anyone but ourselves. Not only was she the face of the Trinity, Julie was now hailed as 'The Face' and 'The Voice' in her own right. All too soon she was peering from the pages of *Harper's* and *Vogue*, bedecked in feather boas and Ossie Clark designs and glammed to the absolute nines. Julie personified the Seventies before the Seventies had even kicked off. There was something heart-rending in the way she talked about all this behind closed doors, away from the cameras that were now prying relentlessly into her life. She hated the drive to portray her as a babe and a dolly girl. It wasn't her. Julie had balls, she was one of the boys, she knew her place in the band. She also defied pigeon-holing. But that didn't stop the media. There were set ways in which to portray women, and that was that. Despite her protests, in an interview in weekly music magazine *Disc*, that she wasn't a sex symbol, they persisted in packaging her as one. Our management were delighted. We got invited to plenty of parties on the back of Julie's popularity. I got to know the Bee Gees as a result.

But I wasn't a pop star. I was a bass player. The limelight wasn't on me. Brian was always saying that I looked bemused by our sudden breakthrough. I would stand around at those pretentious pop parties feeling like the classic Yuletide greetings card illustration: a starved, shoeless Victorian urchin in the street on Christmas Eve, peering through windows at the revellers and their feasts. The image seemed ominous. Was All This what I really wanted to be doing with my life? It suddenly occurred to me how much I missed art. I missed my painting. I did at one point begin drawing a cartoon strip, 'The Four Knobs', but band commitments deprived me of the time to take it further. We seemed to be always on the road or in a television studio. We appeared with the Bee Gees on Frankie Howerd's show, we did Peter Cook and Dudley Moore's *Goodbye Again*, and performed 'Season of the Witch' in a sauna. We were supposed to do a six-week residence on David Frost's *Frost on Sunday*, but that was somehow whittled down to two appearances. We'd get whisked off to Europe to do German TVs. At a festival in Essen, we shared a bill with Frank Zappa's Mothers of Invention and folk-rock supremo Tim Buckley. We were everywhere and nowhere, baby. It was the problem. I began to feel more like a pair of hands affixed permanently to a bass guitar than a functioning human being. All that endless despatching us round the world and dropping us on stage in front of animated crowds did nothing to reassure me otherwise. I started to lose my mind to the cause – or did I? I remember us doing a show in a circus tent somewhere, I'm not sure where exactly, and looking out into the audience to see a be-caped Salvador Dalí staring back at me. That *was* him, wasn't it? Or was that me seeing things after having smoking too much dope? I admit, I had succumbed to the drug lately: partly because everyone else was doing it, but mainly because it opened a portal into a more heightened musical experience that was perfect for the Trinity's sonic explorations. Perhaps it was merely a way of coping with the madness.

Every hit demands a sequel. Should I say, the record company demands it. For our follow-up, Julie favoured 'Road to Cairo', a melancholy dirge by gifted American singer-songwriter David Ackles.

This world-weary sob was perfect for her voice, we all agreed. We set to it. Our manager Gomelsky produced what turned out to be a stunning, lavishly-orchestrated record, with Brian ripping the throat out of the organ, mellotron and harpsichord, a suicidal swelling from the brass section and an unprecedented lament from Julie to take the piece to its mournful climax. We'd done it again, with a song which seemed to sum up the prevailing mood. Where once all you needed was love, the world was now wading through the swamps of despair, and was demanding music to do it to.

Maybe our cover of the song was a touch too classy, and its subject matter too gloomy to match 'This Wheel's On Fire''s success. Perhaps Brian was right, and the song came out too late to capitalise properly on 'This Wheel's's huge success. Even the promotion we did for it ran into difficulties. Julie embarrassed herself during her interview on *The Eamonn Andrews Show*, shrugging indifferently throughout, which was not like her. This wasn't, however, bad manners. The poor girl was simply exhausted. It was obvious to the rest of us that she'd had enough, and that she was desperate to get off the merry-go-round. The incessant schedule of TVs, radios, gigs and interviews had taken its toll. When *The Eamonn Andrews Show* console malfunctioned and we didn't get to play the song, it felt like an omen. The record didn't even make the Top Thirty.

One thing led to another. Dissatisfaction all round. I think we all wanted out, not just Julie. But we had built a profile across Europe and into Scandinavia, as far as Czechoslovakia. We had performed at the Berlin Jazz Festival, where we were 'acclaimed'. A breakthrough in America was within our grasp. Somehow we all sat tight, kept our traps shut and waited to see what would happen. Stoned out of my brains most of the time by now, I couldn't read the writing on the wall, so was unperplexed. When Gomelsky approved a Trinity album minus Julie, I barely flinched.

Definitely What!, recorded at Advision Studios, was engineered by Eddie Offord, the future prog rock mechanic behind Yes and ELP. It was a perfect fit, given that this new LP was our most progressive ever. It opened with a massive instrumental version of the Beatles' 'A Day In the Life', which we'd been performing live for quite a while. There were also Brian Auger originals and some covers of Wes Montgomery, Mose Allison and Booker T. Brian was in his element and taking back control of his baby. He was obviously glad to see the back of our singer for a while. But when we gathered to listen to the playback, the truth whacked us all in the face. As good as we were on this LP, as tight as we sounded, as experimental as it proved us to be, we were nothing without Julie.

15

DAYDREAM BELIEVER

Jack Good, he who had produced the late Fifties music shows *Six-Five Special* for the BBC and *Oh Boy!* for ITV, and who had created a hugely-successful Beatles Special in the early Sixties, was now a big television cheese in the United States. Having produced series such as *Shindig!*, and after helping to break Sonny & Cher, he had now reverted to his Special thing again, and was making one about the Monkees. It was to be called *33⅓ Revolutions Per Monkee*, and he wanted us to be in it. Jack himself auditioned us, in an office off Leicester Square. Julie and Brian read through some pages of scripted dialogue, hamming it up like a comedy duo, which prompted a 'fucking good!' It was praise indeed from the famously reticent Jack. We were hired, and we were going to California.

Jack took an instant shine to me. He soon revealed that he had other, special plans for me. He took our drummer Clive Thacker and me out to dinner one night, to elaborate on them. In a beautiful Malibu restaurant looking out over the Pacific, he outlined his idea for me to star as Roderigo in his latest ambitious project: a modern, musical adaptation of *Othello* called *Catch My Soul*, which would be set in a commune. As you will no doubt appreciate, I was beside myself.

The Monkees show would feature Brian and Julie as evil sorcerers who kidnap the Monkees and transform them into a brainwashed pop combo, who would in turn convert the entire population. A cross between a farce and a nightmare, it would revive Brian as Darwin, the band members as apes, and deliver a balletic variation on the theme of *The Origin of Species* to be going on with. Who on earth dreamed these things up? We performed two songs, the Young Rascals' 'Come On Up' and our take on the Monkees' own 'I'm A Believer', complete with Julie duetting with Mickey Dolenz. When Mickey sang the word 'face' during the chorus, the camera zoomed in on 'The Face', aka our Julie.

The finale commenced with a close-up on Brian at his Hammond organ. The camera then zoomed to reveal Brian on top of Jerry Lee Lewis, playing his piano beneath him. Out a bit and we had Lewis on top of Little Richard. Out a bit more and Little Richard was riding Fats Domino. Still with me? Cut to a Fifties-style revue, with all the guests playing a rock'n'roll medley. Brian as cheesy compere introduced the Monkees, now in the guise of a Four Seasons-inspired vocal group. Fats and Jerry Lee were in sequins, Little Richard dazzling in reflective squares. Brian and Julie were then evil sorcerers again, declaring that the whole thing had been a huge mistake. The raucous climax was a jam for all on the abandoned soundstage, with random props and jukeboxes. Our audience was a bunch of hippies plucked at random from Sunset Strip, after Jack had sent a bus to do a trawl there. An open book superimposed over the mayhem now thumped shut, its cover reading, 'The Beginning of the End'. The credits rolled. The nukes exploded. What was all that about?

We bonded with the Monkees. We hung out at all their houses and round their pools. Nice guys. They were much greater than the sum of their manufactured-pop-star parts. Davy Jones and Mickey Dolenz had both been child actors. Peter Tork was a Greenwich Village folkie and was, like Michael Nesmith, a serious musician. I hadn't realised that before I met them. They were easy-going guys, and were pleasant to work with. But their Special was plagued with problems. We hadn't realised, when shooting began, that the Monkees had only just arrived back from a gruelling Australian tour. They were exhausted. A union strike sent the producers flapping for an alternative soundstage (they secured one at MGM Studios). They also had problems with us. They were collectively miffed that Jack had showcased us in ways that eclipsed them, the supposed stars of the show. Tork walked, after we wrapped. He quit the band. He'd monkeyed around enough.

Our show was aired on NBC in April 1969, but clashed with the televised Oscars. BBC2 showed it in the UK a month later, where it didn't go down well. What was this monstrosity? Far from being received as the slice of zany entertainment it was intended to be, it came across as an act of pop star sabotage. A manufactured group tearing their own fabricated image to shreds, and poking fun at the industry which had made them could hardly be called self-satire. Self-destruction, more like. It bombed.

The Monkees split, the show was aired in the wrong sequence (not that a casual viewer would have noticed) and there were no more Monkees Specials. Jack Good moved swiftly on to stage his *Othello* adaptation, minus me as his Roderigo. PP Arnold and PJ Proby featured instead, along with rock group the Gass. *Catch My Soul* failed to capture the imagination of the critics, but the audiences loved it. It was made into a feature film five years later. Jack would convert to Catholicism and devote himself to religious painting, denouncing the television industry as 'the Devil'. Watching that mad Monkees Special, one could only concur.

At least we ended 1968 on a high, topping a number of end-of-year polls. The *Melody Maker* Pop Readers' Poll voted us the 'Brightest New Hope'. Julie was 'Best Girl Singer', and 'This Wheel's On Fire' was only just beaten by the Stones' 'Jumpin' Jack Flash' as the year's 'Best Single'. Brian did well in the non-Pop poll as third-best organist. We had made a start at breaking America, never mind that it was linked to the outgoing Monkees. We had a US tour pencilled for 1969. How was that supposed to work, now that Brian and Julie were not getting on? What did I know?

Another year, another album. Julie was back on the case, for *Streetnoise*. There wasn't much time in which to compose and record, only a fortnight, in fact, but we got on with it. The sessions took place at our favourite studio, Advision. We soon had enough material for the latest thing, a double album, which was more than enough to satisfy both Brian and Julie. There was even a little room for me to sing one of my own compositions, 'In Search of The Sun'. The song poured out of me one night, its lyrics brimming with violence, loneliness and despair. How troubled I must have been, to have penned such a thing. I wish to this day that I hadn't recorded it. We played it in the wrong key for my voice, and I still can't bear to listen to it. Apart from that, *Streetnoise* was a triumph. Perhaps the biggest surprise of the LP was Julie's own work. 'Vauxhall to Lambeth Bridge', 'A Word About Colour' and 'Czechoslovakia' were outstanding songs and remarkably mature pieces. Their subject matter was a departure, demonstrating serious introspection and political conscience.

Our take on Richie Havens's 'Indian Rope Man' was selected by Gomelsky for release as a single. We did all the usual TV promotion, Tom Jones's show in the UK, Germany's *Beat Club*, but it wasn't a hit. Which didn't bother the rest of the band. Brian expressed, in an interview with the *Melody Maker*, little concern for chart success. We were 'serious artists', not Cliff Richards. That again. As much as the whole notion of pop fame and fortune baffled me, I loved a pop tune as much as the next guy. I found our catchy, edgy singles as good as anybody's. Unbeknown to me, the rest of the group did not agree with me.

But there was no denying the fact that album-oriented rock was now considered to be superior to the pop single. It was where the Trinity's destiny lay. *Streetnoise* was reviewed most favourably by critic Lester Bangs in *Rolling Stone* magazine, who deemed us to be as intelligent as San Francisco's Jefferson Airplane with a 'down home' feeling when required. It was just what we needed to galvanise us for our American tour to come. We hit the ground running, performing in New York, Philadelphia and Chicago. The reception all over was ecstatic. Our audiences greeted us with levels of screaming and applause that we simply hadn't expected. At New York's Fillmore East, we were the only act other than Hendrix to perform two encores.

In Chicago, my hotel room was invaded by Cynthia Albritton and her infamous Plaster-Casters, seeking to set my erect organ (as opposed to my bass) in plaster for posterity. Once I'd stopped laughing enough to realise they were not joking, I pointed them at the band-mates more likely to oblige. I was less shy with the groupies who never left us alone on the road. What the hell, Sue and I now practically hated each other.

We headed west, and opened for our old mate Jimmy Page's Led Zeppelin at the Pasadena Rose Palace and in San Francisco. At last, I started pinching myself. I was twenty-four years old, in a band, touring America, playing alongside some of the biggest names on the planet. Apart from the issue of domestic crisis back home, which I had parked for the time being, things could not be going much better. But I didn't know the half of it, and was unprepared for the pyrotechnics when Giorgio Gomelsky turned up. Brian and Julie had pleaded with our manager to stay away and leave us to it. He came out anyway. It was all downhill from there. Brian was sick and tired of the way that Gomelsky was handling us. We'd been overbooked, the shows were too close together, the travel arrangements were too tight and were mismanaged, and the pressure was all too much. Julie was exhausted, and had had enough. Giorgio turning up out of the blue when he was under strict instructions not to sent the pair of them over the edge.

So they quit. That was it.

As great as it had been watching the freaks on Sunset Strip, a sinister sense of things slipping out of control hung heavily in the air. We were constantly being reminded to be wary of food and drinks, as they were frequently spiked. One evening on Malibu Beach, a member of our entourage lost control and walked into the sea, trying to drown himself. There was a dark side to California, and the scales had fallen from my eyes.

In an attempt to escape the madness, drummer Clive and I went up to San Francisco to see Judy Wong, a close friend of Fleetwood Mac whom I'd known since our Shotgun Express days. Like everyone else we were exhausted, and needed to chill out for a while. We attended a free concert featuring the Grateful Dead and Jefferson Airplane. As the sun set over the valley, all I could see were countless groups of naked bodies, frolicking happily as if they didn't have a care in the world. It was like watching the sun go down on a future that would never come to pass.

No sooner had Julie left the band than *Streetnoise* entered the American charts. We had broken America just as we were breaking up. Which the rest of us were doing slowly.

We still had the Bilzen Jazz Festival to play that summer. A few old band members came back. Further music was recorded. Brian had rediscovered his mojo, but I had lost my own enthusiasm. The new 'improved' Trinity was too much of a departure for me. The magic had gone out of it.

I let my hair grow long. I developed a taste for pot. I even got around to dropping acid for the first time, on stage one night at London's Camden Roundhouse. All of which was a reaction to what Brian Auger's Trinity had turned into. All I wanted was to play pop songs like 'This Wheel's On Fire' again. But I was out of time. As were the Trinity. We weren't the only ones. Brian Jones was found face-down in his pool, and the rock'n'roll corpses started piling up. Jimi Hendrix, Jim Morrison and Janis Joplin died too, between 1969 and 1971. All four of them were twenty-seven years old.

John Lennon left the Beatles in September 1969. Paul McCartney announced they were finished in April 1970. Peter Green left Fleetwood Mac, the group that had soared to unimaginable heights with a new guitarist and songwriter, Danny Kirwan, but without me. Peter's questing, spiritual music had voyaged way beyond Brit-blues homage. It had inspired the Beatles and had reached the West Coast, stimulating American bands to greater heights. During the decade to come, Fleetwood Mac would relocate there, and would reinvent themselves yet again. Would anyone remember the name Peter Green? I doubt he would have cared.

I always wanted to get back and play with him again. Sadly, I never got the chance.

In 1975, just after Pete B. and his wife Julia had been putting him up for a while, Peter came to stay with us in Fulham (by which time I was married to my second wife Angie, of whom more later). It was only then that we realised how ill he was. The gossip and rumours about how he had become so are conflicting. My understanding is that, in 1970, the band had been in Munich among a bunch of jet-set Beautiful People, who lured them back to some aristo-type commune where it was all going on. It was there, so I'm told, that Peter ingested the hallucinatory drug 'Orange Sunshine': otherwise known as ALD-52, one of the most powerful mescalines in existence. It is comparable to LSD, and you have to be very careful indeed who you take it with. I took it myself, so I knew first-hand. The band apparently drifted off, having decided that they didn't care for the Beautiful People. They left Greenie to it, and that's what he wound up getting involved in. Knowing him, he probably thought it would lead him to deep inspiration. Being a true artist, he believed he had to experiment to reach the core of himself and harness his fundamental creativity. It has been said down the years that his drink was spiked, that he was unaware that he had taken it, that someone else had been responsible for the damage. But I think he must have taken it deliberately. I'm sure, in fact, that he wanted to, convinced that it would help him to discover things. But as with all such substances, take it with the wrong people and the outcome can be disastrous. In Greenie's case, it led to a massive breakdown.

Pete and Jules Bardens asked us if we could put Greenie up for a few days, as he was basically living on friends' sofas, with no home of his own. While he was staying with us, it became very apparent that he needed expert psychiatric help. He was refusing to wear any clothes, and would only eat cake. After two or three days, Angie had had enough: I was at work, and she was on her own all day with Peter. We decided, along with Peter B, to take him on a boat trip down the Thames. So we hired a motor boat and travelled up and down the river, soaking up the warm summer sunshine and trying to encourage Greenie to get help. But he was very detached from us all. It was clear that the time had come. In the end, after some persuasion from me, he agreed to go and see someone. We heard through the grapevine that he had done so, and that he had been admitted to a psychiatric hospital. Sad times.

After that, we didn't see him again for a long time. We'd hear stories about him being holed up in a cave in Granada, Spain, and that he was living and playing in Sacromonte: the fabled gypsy community up on the hills opposite the Alhambra. It was the kind of place that attracted musicians, artists and misfits from all over the world. Exactly Greenie's kind of place, Angie and I agreed. We later heard that he had found his way back to England, was living in Hastings, and that he'd got married and had a child. The marriage didn't last long, maybe less than a year. It didn't surprise me.

He was arrested after he allegedly threatened David Simmons, his accountant, with a shotgun. This was all to do with Peter's attitude to money. Greenie once told me that my father, 'the Prof', had been a very big influence on him. My dad used to give a lot of money away to various causes, and Greenie thought that was a good idea. He hated the thought of musicians playing for commercial gain. As far as he was concerned, music had to be pure, and for its own sake, untainted by filthy lucre. He wanted the whole band to give all their money away to a string of charities.

He did get a little better, and did start recording again. From 1979, there were a number of solo albums. He also contributed to Fleetwood Mac's album *Tusk*, on the track 'Brown Eyes', though he wasn't credited in the sleeve notes. He recorded with Mick Fleetwood again, on Mick's solo work, and did a considerable number of sessions.

I was very pleased to hear that they included him in the Rock and Roll Hall of Fame induction for Fleetwood Mac in 1998, soon after which people started talking about the original line-up getting back together. That didn't happen, but Peter did start recording and touring again about ten years ago.

The last time I saw him was in 2002, in the restaurant at Nomis Studios on Sinclair Road, Hammersmith. Once a major rehearsal complex created by music business manager Simon Napier-Bell, it was by then the headquarters of the Sanctuary Music Group. Greenie spotted me, came over and sat down. I was thrilled to see him. 'How are you?' I asked. 'I'm doing a band here, we're rehearsing,' he said. 'I really want to see you play, Dave. I need to hear some new songs from you.' He started laying into me because I was no longer a musician, but had crossed over to 'the other side'. 'Actually,' I said, 'I *am* writing and playing.' I started telling him all about my latest project, Dark Nebula. He was delighted. His face lit up and his eyes glistened with tears. He was so glad to hear that I still had the music in me. He had heard it from the horse's mouth, and he was satisfied. He urged me to keep on playing. I promised him that I would. Because of him, I play to this day. We bid each other goodbye on a high that day. It was the last time I ever saw him.

On 25th February 2020, Mick staged a tribute concert to Peter at the London Palladium. Greenie himself was conspicuous by his absence. When I heard that he'd been found dead only five months later, on 25th July, it really unsettled me. I paced about for several days afterwards. I was upset that he'd gone, but so very glad that he'd lived. I was relieved that he'd been taken in his sleep. The best way. As befitting a gentle man, which he truly was: perhaps the gentlest man I have ever known. He was one of the greatest blues guitarists this country has ever produced. We are unlikely to see his like again. His brilliance, though feted, was largely unsung. The more I think about that, the more I reckon there's something right about it.

★

Julie Driscoll recorded a solo album called *1969* that was released in 1971. She starred in a TV play called *Season of the Witch*, about the quest for an alternative life. She married Keith Tippett, of free-jazz group Centipede. She spoke eloquently in interviews about the search for her own 'ethnic' music, ever mindful of the fact that her recordings of soul, blues and R&B involved mining the legacies of other artists. Brian Auger formed a band called Oblivion Express. With a name like that, he clearly wasn't bothered about having chart hits. The two came together again in 1977, for old times' sake, when they recorded the album *Encore*.

I still think about the Trinity. We were seriously good musicians. Why did we fail? One, because we should have written more of our own songs, existing as we did during an era when writing and composing were paramount. Two, because we were managed by a highly-creative individual who was, unfortunately, a control freak; who spent far too much time interfering in our internal dynamics while failing to take care of our day-to-day affairs. Goodbye, Giorgio. See you on the flipside.

The Sixties were over. From the coffee shops of dingy Soho basements to the glistening pleasure palaces of California, what a wondrous magic carpet ride it had been.

*1. With Sandy at the family home in
Calcott Street, Notting Hill, 1962*

2. 1st Rubgy 15 at school
(DA back row, 3rd left)

3. With Swiss cousin Denise and
Grandmother in Geneva, March 1968. The
striped jacket was a gift from Mick Fleetwood

4. Bonding with 'the General'
(Angie's father), 1974

I COULD FEEL THE WHOLE WORLD TURN ROUND

CURTAINS ★ FUNNY 'COS NEITHER COULD I ★★ INDIAN THING ★★★★★

THE SHOTGUN EXPRESS

RICKY-TICK HARPENDEN PUBLIC HALL. THURSDAYS

1 SEPT ZOOT MONEY

8 SEPT SHOTGUN EXPRESS ROD STEWART, BERYL MARSDEN

15 SEPT JOHN MAYALL

22 SEPT SHEVELLS

6. Press shot at Amsterdam, 1968
©Alamy

5. The Peter B's, left to right:
Peter Green, Dave Ambrose, Mick Fleetwood, Pete Bardens
Below: As drawn by Pete Bardens

2. 1st Rubgy 15 at school
(DA back row, 3rd left)

3. With Swiss cousin Denise and
Grandmother in Geneva, March 1968. The
striped jacket was a gift from Mick Fleetwood

4. Bonding with 'the General'
(Angie's father), 1974

1. With Sandy at the family home in Calcott Street, Notting Hill, 1962

7.
Top: *The Trinity in 1967, left to right:*
Dave Ambrose, Julie Driscoll, Gary Boyle,
Brian Auger, Clive Thacker ©Alamy
Right: *The band in 1968*

8. On stage in Bristol with The Trinity, 1969
©Alamy

9. Angie and David's wedding day, September 1975

10. David's father 'dressed for action'!

11. Christening of firstborn, Katie, 1977

12: Top: the family at Westfield, the home of David's parents
Bottom: David's parents

13. First day at EMI, 1974, briefcase ready for action

14. DA as crew: River Blackwater, Essex, 1976

15. The Sex Pistols with their manager Malcolm MacLaren looking thrilled at the press conference called to announce their signing to EMI in December 1976. They had been spotted by David Ambrose at the 100 Club ©Alamy

16. *Early promo shot of Duran Duran, signed to EMI by David Ambrose*
©*Alamy*

17. *Colin Thurston, producer, mixing Duran Duran*
with DA's daughter Katie enjoying the fun

18. Right: with Andy Warhol,
avid Duran Duran fan

19. Celebration of Duran Duran sales, DA kneeling far right.

20. DA, MD of MCA. 1986, La Quinta

21. *Tollesbury, Essex, at the mouth of the River Blackwater by David Ambrose*

23. David with his sister Philippa

24. 'Our descendants': Barney, Rory, Lauren and Katie, with our grandchildren.

16

IN THE COURT OF
THE CRIMSON KING

What do you do when all else has failed? You go back, cap in hand, to your dad. Mine was at least receptive, and welcomed home his Prodigal Son. He could see that I'd given rock stardom my best shot. He agreed it was hardly my fault that things hadn't worked out. It wasn't as if I hadn't tried. I had assumed that a return to session bass-playing would be a doddle, and that I would still be much in demand. But music, and the industry that supported it, had moved on. A dip into the psychedelic Kingdom Come, the Crazy World of Arthur Brown – he of the four-octave operatic voice, far-out stage shows and the million-seller 'Fire'– during which the God of Hellfire required me to perform dressed as the Pope – convinced me that I wasn't for hire at *any* cost.

My father knew people. He pulled strings. He somehow managed to secure me an interview at EMI Records. The venerable establishment was seeking a label manager for its progressive new imprint Harvest. I donned my best jacket, shirt and tie and did my darnedest to look corporate. I had no idea what to expect that day when I turned up at the Manchester Square building for my appointment, without the foggiest as to what I should say. I remember spouting all manner of nonsense to the interviewer Ron White about free concerts and free recorded music, which of course was hilariously at odds with the aims of a global commercial enterprise. My head was still in the clouds; still swirling with images of the sun going down on a San Francisco love-in with a soundtrack by the Grateful Dead. I was also still doped out of my brains. They didn't hire me. Yet something told me, as I was escorted off the premises, that I would be back.

I joined a few groups, and left a few groups. I lined up with Vinegar Joe, the band that would launch the careers of Robert Palmer and Elkie Brooks. I was welcomed by Spooky Tooth, a great rock act on Island Records. I jammed with Third Ear Band, who created the soundtrack for folk-horror flick *The Wicker Man*. But my heart wasn't in it. I was all burned out. The problem was, I needed a source of income. I'd had plenty of between-bands odd jobs in my time. I'd even cleaned houses, I wasn't proud. Menial work wasn't really my thing, but is it anybody's? Bottom line, I was done with music. Until a record came out that changed my mind.

It was by T. Rex, a band I'd never heard of, and it was called 'Ride a White Swan.' It sounded crisp, catchy and polished, and was a breath of fresh air. It brimmed with contradictions. It harked back to hippiedom and nodded towards a brighter future. Unashamedly pop, it also paid homage to folk music, with its singalong to handclaps and an exam-level guitar solo that seemed to be saying, look, anyone can do this! You could almost smell the patchouli on its singer, Marc Bolan. It was clear to me in that moment that here was the Seventies' first true star. I bought the single and I flipped it over. There on the B-side was a cover of Eddie Cochran's 'Summertime Blues'. My childhood hero must be giving me the nod. I could do *this*! I was still only twenty-four years old, only a year or so older than Bolan. Perhaps this was my wake-up call. Perhaps I could get a job in a band like that.

★

All was anything but quiet on the domestic front. Sue and I had practically fought our way through the walls of the Ifield Road flat. Determined to save our marriage, I decided to look for a new home. With the money I had stashed from our Trinity record company advances, I purchased a sizeable Victorian rectory on Jephtha Road, Putney. It was falling to bits and required extensive renovation, a task I thought would be just the thing to distract me. When it was finished, it would give Sue and me a fresh start. To be fair, she seemed as excited about it as I was. We rolled up our sleeves and got stuck in. We repaired the roof and papered over the cracks. We were doing much the same in our crumbling marriage.

But our new house was never a home. It was more like the film set of a horror movie, something in which Vincent Price might have starred. I even started referring to it as 'the House of Wax', after the 1950s horror thriller of that name. I had expected a transformation after the refurbishment was completed, but there was nothing of the sort. There was only a coldness, an unwelcoming emptiness, that caused me to retreat by myself into rooms I had claimed as 'mine'; where I smoked tons more pot and started reading philosophy, in particular the works of Carl Jung and Marshall McLuhan. I was lost. I didn't have a job to go to. My wife seemed to feel nothing but contempt for me.

The ever-gregarious Sue had found herself a job as a waitress, at the Hungry Years restaurant in Earls Court. She was soon inviting people she met there back to our house. They started staying the night. A number of them became lodgers who never got round to paying rent. I knew things were going off the side when I started waking up to strangers in my bed. Between me and Sue, there would be someone new. Life had become a confusion of ever-changing characters. Who *was* this that I was married to? I barely recognised her anymore. I barely recognised myself. In denial of our dire situation, we threw parties, as if to kid ourselves that everything was all right. Mick Fleetwood and Jenny Boyd would come. Julie Driscoll too.

I missed the music business, or so I thought. Against my better judgement, I joined Robert Fripp's King Crimson, whose music defied both categorisation and common sense, and to which Julie's husband Keith Tippett contributed keys. From day one, I was out of my depth. I couldn't respond to Fripp's dictatorial way of doing things. But I needed to find the strength and commitment from somewhere. In desperation – don't judge me – I called a King's Road type I knew called Psychedelic Paul, who came to the House of Wax to perform an invocation. The general idea was to summon creative energies and reinvigorate my artistic focus. Something like that. At the very least, perhaps it would get me through a King Crimson rehearsal without losing the will to live. All laughable now, of course, but people had funny ideas in those days. I was by no means the only musician who was into black magic. Jimmy Page and David Bowie were obsessed with the occultist and magician Aleister Crowley. Graham Bond even thought he was Crowley's son. Mick Jagger did the soundtrack for a film by Kenneth Anger, another meddler in the so-called Dark Arts. Peter Gabriel chronicled an otherworldly evening on the Genesis song 'Supper's Ready' from their 1972 album *Foxtrot*. What was probably drug-addled delusion and/or compromised mental health seemed very real at the time. However ludicrous it might sound now, I believed in spells.

Because it worked. I was convinced of it. Not that it made me more committed to King Crimson. Its effect was to make me start painting frantically, as though my life depended on it. I became prolific, and lost all sense of time. I completely forgot that Fripp was still expecting me to turn up to rehearsals and play bass. He called me eventually, to ask if I was ever coming back. My explanation – that a warlock had put a spell on me – was met with stony silence. I had talked myself into becoming King Crimson's ex-bass player.

Suffice it to say, my revelation was met initially with an awkward silence and the conversation didn't last much longer.

I fretted around the place for a few days, wondering what on earth to do next. I needed a job. I was desperate for income. I told myself, yet again, that I had to move on from music. It was time to take my responsibilities seriously, and to grow the fuck up.

I became a door-to-door salesman.

I responded to an ad in the *Evening Standard* offering 'Bread for Heads': which meant 'money for switched on, cool people' in the parlance of the day. I went along to Hollywood Road in Chelsea, round the corner from our old flat, to find an animated young man by the name of Chris Salewicz giving a talk on the art of selling works of art by knocking on people's front doors. The velvet paintings in question were by no means exquisite. They were gaudy black velvet backdrops featuring brightly-coloured subjects. Madonna and Child, a galleon, a kitten, a Masai warrior. They made Vladimir Tretchikoff's 'Chinese Girl', that ridiculed 1950s painting so ubiquitous in Seventies suburban living rooms, look like Caravaggio. I thought of my training at the Byam Shaw, and almost hung my head in shame.

I needed the money. I took the job. The enthusiasm of salesman Chris was infectious. He was fresh out of university, a staunch socialist, and all for ripping off the middle classes: the phrase that he would utter to me before we set off for suburbia in the van. We drove from Wimbledon to Bromley to Rickmansworth, flogging our terrible tat. Bored housewives were easy prey, and we were ruthless. I hadn't expected to enjoy the work: the art was ugly, our enterprise more so. But I soon cottoned on to the arts of the spiel and the deal, and found it all quite exhilarating. There is a certain skill in talking people into buying things they don't need. My eyes were opened widely to the public's penchant for bad taste.

Only with hindsight did I realise that the flogging of crap art equipped me with all the skills I required to work in a record company.

There was the all-important first impression: that initial engaging with the person who answered the door. Sometimes they'd slam it in your face, but you didn't let it get to you. You simply knocked on the one next-door. The next trick was to get yourself invited in. You'd flatter them, admire their décor. If they wanted to talk about their problems, as they so often did, you listened sympathetically and sometimes told them about your own. You'd then ask if they'd watched whatever sitcom had been on the night before. You then pulled a picture from your portfolio, reminding them that they'd seen it before, in that show, last night, that it was on the wall of the main character's lounge. You invited them to stroke the lovely velvet. You walked around their home, pointing out bits of wall where it might hang. You sometimes kidded them that you'd created this priceless work yourself. I never went as far as that, but you get the picture (as it were). Not that I would have put my name to any one of those crass pieces. I still had a little integrity.

The bizarre thing was that, more often than not, you made the sale. I started making money. Sue was happy. The couple who ran the business expanded, with other art products for us to sell, which were basically fake antiques. Still, I enjoyed the work much more than I had anticipated. I got on well with Salewicz. He couldn't believe that I'd jacked in my music career to sell fake art door-to-door. He introduced me to Roxy Music, a band I quickly fell in love with. They sounded fantastic, and were not so far removed from the rock'n'roll I had escaped. They seemed to occupy, with David Bowie, the upper echelons of the movement T. Rex had started with their single 'Ride A White Swan'. Bolan's band were now huge with a string of hits to their name, while Bowie and Roxy were glitter rock with a difference.

Chris soon grew bored of the life of a door-to-door salesman, and reinvented himself as a journalist with the *NME*. I stayed behind and kept on flogging the crap art, until I really looked at a couple of the prints one slow day. I noticed some text peeping out. It dawned on me that the pictures had probably been torn out of art history books. I could do that myself. Why didn't I?

I was soon up and running with my own business, The Beau Vista Fine Arts Club, selling reproductions of classic, tasteful paintings. I bought my prints from the National Gallery. I did well to begin with. We even featured in an exhibition at Earl's Court. Then we started getting complaints from customers that the pictures were disintegrating. Another commercial lesson had been learned: you can sell people shit for a bit, but don't be surprised when they start to notice. Fortunately, the shelf life of a pop group is significantly longer than the time it takes for a dodgy Rembrandt knock-off to decay. It is sometimes.

With nothing to do and no particular place to go, I decided to head for the Mecca of lapsed hippies facing the inevitable mid-life crisis. They'd all been there. It was the done thing in those days, a rite of passage. If it was good enough for Winston Churchill, the Stones and the Beatles, it was good enough for me. It seemed exotic, other-worldly, the perfect place to which to escape: a hedonistic epicentre of opium and dope, and just the spot to 'sweep the cobwebs from the edges of my mind'. It was according to Crosby, Stills and Nash, at least.

I booked myself a package to Marrakech. I'm not sure how I got away with it – the Sue I remember would never have allowed it – but somehow I went alone.

17

ESCAPISM

What did you do in Marrakech, Dave? I did exactly what everybody else did in those days. I wasted time, hung with the hippies, smoked some dope, played a little guitar. I came back convinced that my life had to change; that my marriage was screwed; that I should devote the rest of my life to art and music.

I returned from the heat and the sand to the frost and hostility of the House of Wax. I took to my garden, making 'art' out of anything I could find, anything to take my mind off things. I talked myself, against the odds, into the Royal College of Art. I took up my bass again. I resumed writing songs. I joined another band, a pub rock group by the name of WH Pearce, whose ad I had come across in one of the papers. Their guitarist, Martin Glover, became my friend. We gigged around the circuit as often as we could get booked, and I felt reborn. None of which I had discussed with my wife. I justified this glaring oversight by reminding myself that she had her own life. She had her job, her friends, her family, her own world, none of which included or affected me. The realisation jolted me: we didn't even care about each other anymore. We were a pair of strangers who happened to be living under the same roof. What a state of affairs. It soon would be.

None of which was reflected in my new songs. Writing became my great escape. The kind of thing I was churning out now was a throwback to my Sixties heyday. These latest harked back to Hendrix, Buffalo Springfield and Pink Floyd. They were songs that were inspired by the light and madness of Marrakech, and by the darkness and doom of the House of Wax. I was proud of them. I played them to guitarist Martin Glover. He seemed blown away. He said as much. I was encouraged. We hatched a plan. WH Pearce were as good as finished. We'd keep the drummer, Lucas Cox, and would launch a new band instead. We would call ourselves Dark Nebula, like the interstellar cloud, the name of which we had found in the pages of a comic book.

I used to drive Martin home from gigs. He stayed with us one night, at the House of Wax. When I saw him the next morning, he told me he thought that the house was haunted. He had been disturbed by very dark dreams, during which the house had appeared to distort and invert. As we hadn't indulged in any drugs the night before, I was inclined to take him seriously. It was a relief to hear from someone else that all was not right with the old place. Maybe there *were* malevolent forces coming between my wife and me. Despite Dark Nebula's sure-fire ascent – we had killer songs, monster riffs and good intentions, how could we possibly fail? – my disintegrating marriage continued to torment me. I decided to do what I always did when things became too much. I went to see my dad. The advice he gave me was not at all what I'd been expecting. He told me that I should take some LSD.

On what basis, I couldn't help but wonder. Dad reassured me. It was supposed to be very beneficial to those suffering emotional turbulence, he explained. It could 'unlock the beasts of my subconscious,' and could set me free.

Crikey. Had he been reading Aldous Huxley? I could hardly imagine my father trying LSD for himself. I'd had only the one experience of it, that odd night at Camden Roundhouse with the Trinity, which had not been enough to make me want to try it again. But perhaps Dad had a point. A dash of hallucinogens might just be the thing to bring me to my senses. I went off in search of some Orange Sunshine, which was rumoured to be rather strong. I didn't use it for a while, but kept it in my pocket, awaiting the appropriate moment to give it a go. That moment came when I was driving Martin home to his flat in South Croydon flat one afternoon, after a rehearsal. I put it to him that we should take it together. He didn't take much convincing. Tucked away in his flat, in the company of his female flatmates, we all dropped some Sunshine and sat listening to Stevie Wonder's *Talking Book*. It was amazing. The drug had the effect of enlarging and enhancing every word, every note. We put another record on the turntable and lit a few candles. Then we started seeing things. Giant spiders crawled across the walls. Their upstairs neighbour turned into a skeleton. We needed fresh air, we knew, and ran outside to go for a walk. At the cricket ground, we stupidly climbed onto the roof of the pavilion and walked across it. The sky above us was vast, the view of the city ridiculously large and ominous. We were the only people on the entire planet. I stood for a moment, feeling exposed and regal, like a rock star who had just walked out on stage to play the greatest gig of his life, of anybody's life, only to find that the audience hadn't come. We got down.

I don't remember how I made it back to the House of Wax. I hid myself away in one of the rooms I'd been using, and stared at some pictures I had pinned to the wall. They'd been taken by the photographer Keith Morris during our Ifield Road days. As I sat there studying them, the figures in the images came to life. They leapt from the wall to float and dance above me in the now glowing room. Then they vanished. I glanced back at the wall to see nothing but pictures, lifeless mementos of happier times. I started to cry. I never did acid again.

We performed our first Dark Nebula gig at Royal Holloway University in Egham, Surrey, sharing a set with a band called Ocean. I was a bundle of nerves, not least because I was also now the singer. But I needn't have worried. We were a success, somehow. The crowd adored us. We chatted to some of the audience afterwards, who seemed amazed that we hadn't yet released any records, nor landed ourselves a record deal. The time had come to commit our music to tape. We booked ourselves into Holborn's Budget Studios, where Bowie and Bolan had both recorded. So the man said, anyway. The long story short, it didn't go that well. A lost opportunity. I told myself there would be another time.

★

Back home, Sue had imported a live-in lover. He was one of the chefs at the Hungry Years. I couldn't take this. I confided in one or two friends, and said I was going to move out. They warned me that I must do no such thing. If I walked away from my own house, Sue

131

would assume ownership and I would lose everything I'd worked for. I sat tight, putting up with a situation that was utterly intolerable, an imposter in my own home. Sue's lover, an imposing chap, treated me with utter contempt. I hadn't by any means been an angel myself, but I didn't deserve this.

I went down to Mick Fleetwood's place in Hampshire, a huge house called Benifolds. Twenty rooms, eight acres, completely secluded, woods all round, with its own recording studio on the premises. The Mac would make four albums there. John McVie and his wife Christine had lived there too. They'd suffered considerable upheaval since Peter Green had left. The inter-band drama that turned them into a musical soap opera years before *Rumours* had already commenced. Not that the world was ready for it. Their post-Peter Green material wasn't selling.

I found Mick in a reflective mood, but indefatigable. They had a new American guitarist, Bob Welch, who floated the idea of relocating to California. We talked about that, and then we jammed for a while. It was brilliant to play with Mick again. I left him and Jenny wistfully.

★

Imagine me working as an attendant at the Institute of Contemporary Arts. I did it partly because I needed the money, but mostly because it took me away from home. I enjoyed it. I was inspired by the art all around me, and I was soon promoted to picture hanger. It was there that I happened to run into an old acquaintance from the Byam Shaw: a woman called Verge. Also working at the ICA was her rather beautiful young friend Angela. Angie and I started eyeing each other up. Angie was looking for a place to live. Could I put her up? I thought about it. Angie was a pretty, fashionable, fun-loving chick who liked to laugh her head off and who seemed thrilled to be alive. I didn't take much nudging to offer her a room.

I took Angie back to the House of Wax, and showed her around. We were getting on well, so I asked her to stay and watch some television with me. The next thing I knew, Sue had stormed into the sitting room and was switching channels. It was *her* house and *her* television, she spat. Angie and I were gobsmacked. Sue and I began to argue, furiously. We took the fight outside, into the hall. I suddenly felt something crash onto my back, and I hit the deck with an almighty thud. Sue's gigantic lover had jumped the full flight of stairs, and had landed on me. How he didn't kill me, I'll never know. Against the odds, I picked myself up and managed to stumble away in one piece, towards Angie. I was mortified by what had just happened, and told her I didn't think she should move in. She didn't lose it with me for wasting her time. She just looked at me with a warmth and understanding that had been missing from my life for as long as I could remember. She smiled softly, and said she didn't think I should be there either. She suggested that we leave together. Out of nowhere, she and I had become 'we'.

We stayed, where else, at her temporary accommodation, in a place called Paradise Lodge. I was on the floor at first, but we soon became lovers. That took me back. I wrote a Dark Nebula song for her, called 'Wizards and Queens'. I thought about divorcing Sue. It became clear within a very short time that Angie wasn't going to put up with all my artistic-musician nonsense. I was going to have to get a proper job.

18

PRETTY VACANT

We were written in the stars. Angie was everything that Sue was not, and I thanked God for her. Being only three years my junior, she had cut her teeth on the same artists and records as me. As an 'army brat', she had spent her early childhood in Egypt, following her father from country to country when he was re-posted every few years. She was proud of her dad, who played an active role in the D-Day Normandy landings, and had helped to liberate the Bergen-Belsen concentration camp in Northern Germany. He was the recipient of a Distinguished Service Order, and left the army as a Major General. By the time Angie was nine, her family had settled in Essex.

Like me, she was a boarding school survivor. She'd worked in publishing and the arts, and had briefly been employed by UNESCO in Paris, where she lived in the Quartier Latin. She was well-travelled, cosmopolitan, spunky, spicy, amusing and intelligent. She knew and relished the London music scene, but she was ready to be a grown-up, put down roots and have a family of her own. She was for me.

All of which demanded of me that I get a proper job.

Sue and I divorced, acrimoniously. There's no such thing as 'they parted amicably,' whatever you've read or seen. We sold the House of Wax and went our separate ways. I was more than happy to see the back of both, despite the fact that she took me for every penny I had. Onwards. I went to see her years later, at a shop she had in Fulham. 'I really miss the rock'n'roll lifestyle,' she moaned. She's now married to an engineer who looks like me.

In 1975, two years after we'd met, Angie and I were married. It was the most beautiful, happy, romantic day. The only cloud on the distant horizon bore the handful of family members on her side who disapproved of their little angel getting hitched to a contemptible divorcé. They didn't come, so who cared.

As for employment, the business of music seemed to be my best bet. There must be something in the industry to which I could turn my hand. Angie and I sat down and wrote letters to every record label we could think of. We needn't have invested so much time and ink. The first person to reply was the first who had ever interviewed me: the executive who'd sent me packing from EMI.

Ron White had gone up in the world. He had graduated from his former role as assistant managing director of EMI Records to assume responsibility for the company's expanding publishing empire. He gave me what he called 'a conservative estimate' of the song titles EMI now owned: about a hundred thousand domestically and a hundred and fifty thousand worldwide. Boosted by the global success of the Beatles, it was still bankrolled by the now-defunct band's continuing vast sales. EMI was still expanding, and publishing was the main aspect of the business in which it was investing. Ron had decided to put me in charge of songbooks. It would be my job to extract the most out of existing compositions, while using my ears to find new songs and songwriters to add to the roster.

What did I know about any of that? Precisely nada. But as always, I was prepared to give it a go. What choice did I have? I didn't even know what song publishing was. But since Ron and I had last met, I'd gone knocking on people's doors, and had flogged a lot of dodgy paintings. I was clearly better at business than I looked, which Ron must have perceived. In any case, how hard could it be? All I had to do was find a few tunes worth whistling, and track down some writers who could provide a regular supply. Ron trusted me. He knew I could do it. Which is how I was hired.

The publishing division of EMI turned out to be an independent operation that did not reside in the Manchester Street HQ, by which I was mildly disappointed. I would not, after all, be going to work every day at the very location where Ringo, George, John and Paul had beamed down into the camera for the cover of 'Please Please Me'. I'd be reporting to Pete Phillips at KPM at the 21 Denmark Street offices. Mere mention of which made my pubes curl.

Denmark Street was 'Tin Pan Alley', the heart of the UK's popular music industry; the very place I had made a beeline for on those very first trips to London. I remembered it as though it were yesterday: checking out records in Dobell's, gazing longingly at the guitars in Selmer's and Macari's on Charing Cross Road. This was the hallowed street on which dreams were made, where songs were bought and sold, where management and agency deals were done, where musicians were fawned over or dismissed as utter crap, received generously or ripped off disgracefully, where chance encounters could make or break a career. This was the whole music business, condensed into a handful of buildings which had seen better days on a nondescript stretch of tatty side street. My old mucker Ray Davies had penned a suitably barbed tribute to the unprepossessing little cut-through. The Kinks' 'Denmark Street' told of cynical publishers fobbing off hopeful songwriters with barbs about their music and their hair. They'd buy their tunes anyway, because 'they hate to be wrong,' and there's always a chance they'll make it onto the hit parade. The track's rattling piano drove home even harder the unpalatable truth: that behind the cloying sentiment of pop songs simmered a cry of stone-hearted hounds, pulling the purse strings. I had become one of them.

Were there songs left to sing? Were there lyrics and melodies left to write? If it hadn't all been done, if originality still existed, would I be able to find any? Put it this way, I'd give it my best shot. My marriage depended on it.

★

Arriving at KPM's 21 Denmark Street offices that first day, I was full of hope but scared shitless. Of course I wanted to fit in and make a good impression as quickly as I could, but how was I supposed to do that? I knew nothing of office culture or politics. I felt like the new boy on the first day of school. In an attempt to come across as cool and well-connected, I'd spent more time than usual on my appearance. I'd washed and dressed carefully and had slicked back my hair, in a lame attempt at looking like Bryan Ferry. I taped a poster of Roxy Music's *Country Life* album on the wall behind my desk, just to make sure. So far, so good. No sooner had the working day begun than an endless stream of new faces began rocking up, introducing themselves, taking me through the ropes, adding to my ever-lengthening list of responsibilities. I was somewhat overwhelmed. I thought back to my rare visits with the Trinity and our manager Giorgio Gomelsky to our then label, Marmalade Records. It had all seemed rather laid-back, a bearable blend of business and pleasure. Recreation on all levels seemed to be encouraged. I glanced around my new office and at the faces of my new colleagues, and realised to my chagrin that there would be no funny business here. This was more like a public library than a record company. We had a pianist who transcribed all the top lines, and a passageway of rooms with old upright pianos. The top lines were then sent to the British Museum for safe keeping. Part of my job was to listen to all the tapes that artists sent in to us. Every single one, because you just never knew. I had to treat every young hopeful who turned up to pitch to us with the same deference as I might greet a Joni Mitchell or a Paul McCartney, for much the same reason. Most of them hadn't a hope in hell. Their songs would be worse than dire. I still had to sit there and let them play, then offer my considered critique. It was my job. Sometimes it got the better of me. My patience would desert me. I'd tell them the truth. This was never a wise move, and could cause all manner of havoc. I was once even threatened with a knife. Not that the poor chap had it in for me personally. Desperation had got the better of him. It struck home to me what a brutal industry this was.

I never did discover my Paul Simon, but I did manage to make my mark. After a year or so, I was moved to EMI Music Publishing on Charing Cross Road, just round the corner. This was a step up, a significant promotion. The head of publishing, my new boss, was a flamboyant wide boy by the name of Terry Slater. He was, like me, a former musician who had defected. He'd written a few decent songs, he'd played with the Everly Brothers, and had worked on the west coast of America. I assumed that we were two of a kind, and that we'd have a lot in common. I couldn't have been more wrong. Terry was everything I wasn't. He was brash, he was loud, he was in-your-face cocksure. With barrow-boy bravado, bullshit and full-on gab, he elbowed his way in, shoved to the front, and made sure that he was photographed cheek to cheek with the stars. He was as cool in the company of Freddie Mercury as taking PG Tips with an East End gangster. I, on the other hand, was everything Terry despised: meek, mild-mannered and middle-class; a posh public schoolboy out of water. My usual style was to hang back, not draw attention to myself, and watch proceedings from a safe distance; which was going to do me no favours in the music industry. I tried to befriend Slater, having clocked that his patronage was key to my survival. I had already worked out that he would seize all the credit for anything worthwhile that I brought in. It was a risk I'd have to take.

While still riding the Beatles wave, EMI had been making their mark during the Seventies too. T. Rex, Cockney Rebel and Queen were all success stories. 'Bohemian Rhapsody' was the latter's latest big triumph. Its success was proof that while you can sense what might be a hit, there's no foolproof way of knowing. It's trial and error, an art, not a science, and nobody really knows. The unexpected successes were what made it thrilling.

The company's progressive imprint Harvest was coming into its own. 1973's *The Dark Side Of The Moon* was a game changer for post-Syd Barrett Pink Floyd, and was a monumental success. At first, I assumed that my time with EMI Music Publishing would be as uneventful as my tenure at KPM. In some ways, pop had hit a brick wall. Pub rock was never destined to dent the charts. The sparkle was going out of Glam. David Bowie had departed for America, where he had discovered Soul. T. Rex had made the most of their moment, but were now in decline. Yes, EMI still had Queen, but such acts were few and far between. Even *Top Of The Pops* was getting boring. There were only so many Bay City Rollers, Pilots and Sailors an audience could take. Hindsight crystallises the problem: recorded music wasn't reflecting our life and times. Who needed bland drivel on the radio when we were beset by strikes, three-day weeks and power cuts; when the IRA were bombing the fuck out of us, when rat-infested rubbish was piling up in the streets, when inflation was through the roof and when there seemed no end to the madness. How could the music industry have been so out of touch? The tapes kept coming and I kept on trolling off to gigs. My wife was pregnant, and I was again in denial.

Terry Slater never went out to see bands. I did all the donkey work. I remember him saying to me, 'Dave, just remember: we're working together. You've got the brains and I've got the bunny!' He had plenty of that, all right. So it was that, at the end of May 1976, I went with Angie to the Nashville Rooms, a decent-sized venue in Fulham where

I would experience U2, Joe Strummer and the Clash, the Stranglers and so many other great acts, to see these young Australian upstarts calling themselves AC/DC. What did *that* mean? The electrical term alternating current/direct current, perhaps? Or that they vacillated sexually? I discovered only later that the brothers had simply seen those letters on the rear of their sister's sewing machine, and had decided that they would make a memorable band name. The moniker was nothing if not symbolic of their explosive energy and unforgettable act. I was enthralled. They were absolutely fantastic, the tightest hard-rock act I'd ever seen. I looked at Angie and mouthed, 'Oh, this is obvious, isn't it!' She was there ahead of me, of course, as she so often is.

Angus was a superb lead guitarist, strutting about in his shorts. He was wearing the whole school-uniform look, even in those days. He had the hair and the torrent of attitude. The band had been going for about three years by then, having been launched by Angus and his rhythm-guitarist brother Malcolm in Australia. Their family had emigrated there from Scotland during the early 1960s. Already hugely popular Down Under, it was now time to conquer the world.

I went in the next day and told Terry all about them. 'Sign 'em!' he cried. 'Fuckin' sign 'em! Let's do it!' They were one of those bands I didn't have to think about. That they were going to be very, very big was written all over them. There was nothing to analyse. No hiccups to overcome. They just *were*. 'Get 'em right,' used to be a catchphrase in the office. But this lot were *already* right. They were perfect just as they were. They would rise to become one of the most successful acts of the early 1980s. At one point they had the third highest-selling album with their future classic *Back in Black*. And *we* had their publishing.

★

Four months later Chris Salewicz called. My former crap-picture-flogging partner-in-crime, now a fully-fledged *NME* journalist, alerted me to a gig at the 100 Club on Oxford Street that night that was going to change my life.

The 'Sex Pistols'? What kind of a name was that? What the hell, in for a penny. It was only when I got to the shabby old jazz club that had fallen on hard times that I sensed something in the air, and knew that this gig was going to be different. I descended the steps into the hellhole. I felt myself drowning in sweat as somebody whacked me over the head with a full-on oven. It certainly felt as though they had.

The quartet of dishevelled rogues who shambled onto the stage looked unimpressive. As soon as they started to play, I changed my mind. It was savage. It was music, yet it was anything but. I hadn't heard such swagger and attitude since the Faces. There was nothing safe or cute about this. It was grotesque. The guitarist was sensational, the bassist solid, and their drummer was bang-smack on the dough. The riffs were brilliant and they were as tight as arseholes. Their sound had an undercurrent of Sixties Mod pop, and an anger that scared the crap out of me. Their versions of the Who's 'Substitute', the Monkees' 'Stepping Stone' and the Small Faces' 'What'cha Gonna Do About It' were more mutilations than covers. The lead singer was Quasimodo on acid: gnarled, deformed, tempestuous, with wild orange hair and a deranged-Alsatian stare. He had the look of a madman with a decayed mouth who might leap from the stage at any moment to tear your head off and devour it whole. He was hostile towards the punters and they were hostile back, gobbing and sneering and chanting obscenities. This lot didn't care. They weren't just ransacking pop, they were shitting all over it.

I stood there gasping with shock. Then I remembered myself. I was a music publisher. There were original songs here the like of which I'd never heard before. Songs encrusted with anarchy, venom and spite, that erupted with bile against the state of the nation and our filth-infested, poverty-stricken times. This wasn't vileness for the sake of vileness. It had a message, which was one that I sensed the common man wanted to hear. How could it fail?

I made enquiries. I met their manager, Malcolm McLaren, who looked as though he could have been the lead singer's dad, except that he was cleaner and somewhat tidier. I read him immediately: an eccentric charmer who would tell me whatever I wanted to hear and be anyone I wanted him to be if it meant bagging his boys a deal. He had me from Fuck Off. We swapped numbers. His card declared that he had a fashion shop on the King's Road, called Sex. He and Vivienne Westwood traded kinky rubber and fetishwear there, apparently, as well as fashion that made M&S look like clerical vestments.

When I got to work the next morning, I practically rugby-tackled Terry with news of my amazing find. He yawned theatrically and scoffed in my face. Call themselves a band, with a name like that? I was having a laugh. Undeterred, I kept pestering. Little by little. Day by day. Terry warmed up. He agreed to give a demo tape five minutes of his valuable time. I did *have* a demo tape, didn't I? No, Terence, alas, I did not. Then suddenly, out of nowhere, I did. A tap on the shoulder and there, as if by magic, was McLaren: standing right in front of me, swishing a wet, devilish smile from lip to lip and brandishing a cassette. How had he got past Security and into the building? Who knew, maybe he walked through walls. Anything was possible.

It was perhaps the roughest demo I'd ever heard, but it captured them perfectly. The Sex Pistols sounded even better on tape than I remembered from their live performance. These were songwriters. 'These' were Johnny Rotten, the festering singer; Glen Matlock, the glaring bassist and primary songwriter; moody guitarist Steve Jones, and drummer Paul Cook. Terry was impressed. He couldn't help himself. Go on, then, he said. He'd check them out.

★

The group had evolved out of the gang that hung around in the shop run by McLaren and Vivienne Westwood, which didn't surprise me. It was the kind of place that attracted outsiders and freaks. They clamoured to get their hands on the weird trousers and ripped T-shirts emblazoned with obscene prints that were sold there. Steve Jones and Paul Cook, the guitarist and the drummer, were regulars. Glen Matlock, having walked out of his Saturday job at Whiteley's department store in Bayswater, was one of the staff, keeping watch over both shoplifters and celebrities. Ken Russell, Ringo Starr, Ian Hunter and Mick Ronson were the kind of celebrities known to shop there. The Sensational Alex Harvey Band had been in for gold socks. McLaren pondered.

Jones and Cook formed a band. Hanging about in the shop one day, they happened upon Glen playing bass. They dubbed themselves the Swankers and then Strand, before somebody hit on the idea of 'Sex Pistols'. Across the pond, McLaren meandered around the Village and found a transvestite group called the New York Dolls. He stumbled across the Ramones, Patti Smith, and Television. Some Yank kids started a fanzine called *Punk*. A lot of energy seemed to be flowing in the same direction.

Back in London, the Sex Pistols started casting around for a singer. One of the contenders was John Lydon, a council estate kid who frequented the shop. Not that he needed to. He'd perfected his look down to the last rip and tear. His image and stance came straight from his wasted heart. He made himself as ugly as possible, because that was how he felt. It was how *life* felt. He auditioned. They snapped him up, but led him to think that they didn't care. His surname gave way to the one that reflected the state of his mouth. Matlock, a St. Martin's College of Art drop-out, pulled strings to get them a gig there. They opened for a band called Bazooka Joe led by Stuart Goddard, who was destined to become Adam Ant. It was hopeless, but word was out. The Pistols appealed to Bowie and Roxy fans. They reeled in the misfits. These kids copied their homemade garb from stuff they'd seen in Sex that they couldn't afford. They made clothes out of bin liners held together with safety pins. Here came the punks.

I went back to see the Pistols again and again at the 100 Club, which unbeknown to us at the time was to become the spiritual home of the punk movement. I took Terry. I took the secretaries. I took the post boys. I even took my heavily pregnant wife. As the Pistols' following increased, so their gigs grew wilder and more outrageous. Bloody fights would break out among the whipped-up audience, the rioting incited by what was going on out there on the streets, and by what was going down on stage. Matlock and Rotten hated each other. It showed. Fucking perfect, declared Terry. It was only a matter of time before we signed them, I felt sure. We had to get a move on if we were going to, however. Once a record deal had been struck, with whichever label, it would be much harder for us to negotiate their publishing deal. EMI Records were weighing them up. Mike Thorne in A&R had been to see them. He was badgering his boss, Nick Mobbs, as relentlessly as I'd been pestering Terry.

All these years later, an impression prevails that the Sex Pistols were Malcolm McLaren's idea, his baby, his perfect creation, just another a manufactured shock-act. Not true. I swear they would have happened anyway. McLaren just happened to be in the right place at the right time, which turned out to be his primary talent. There was such fierce intelligence in the band's songwriting that it couldn't possibly have come from some profit-focused manager. It was too personal, too angry, too *young*. It was the reason why we wanted them. The reason why *I* wanted them, anyway. Their strong, hook-laden songs dripped with emotion and provocation. They were bursting with phrases that resonated, phrases like slogans; like the newspaper-headline songwriting in which John Lennon excelled. Beneath the layers of gob and shit and pinned-together impertinence, these yobs had integrity. They also had a moral conviction that McLaren clearly lacked. More to the point, their following was doubling by the day. All those kids would buy all those Sex Pistols' records. Pound signs were spinning in the eyes and minds of EMI executives like Triple Golds on a slot machine.

As soon as it became apparent that the Pistols were Britain's 'Next Big Thing', Terry Slater's relaxed interest in them went into overdrive. By the time we signed them to our publishing division, for £10,000 in October 1976, I was astonished to find that I'd been airbrushed out of the picture. The photograph commemorating the momentous occasion features Terry with the group, grinning from ear to ear, alongside Malcolm McLaren and his lawyer Stephen Fisher. I am nowhere to be seen. The lesson was a harsh one. If you don't force yourself into what might appear to be insignificant photo opportunities, history will record that you were not even there. Thus did Terry, as predicted, take all the credit for the discovery of the group that my old chum Chris Salewicz had wafted my way. The EMI record company was all set to sign them too. Again, I didn't get a look-in.

It was never plain sailing. The argumentative, angry Pistols railed against everything, from which imprint to put them out on (they were fucked if they were going out on fucking old Harvest, that was a fucking grandads' label, it would be EMI proper or nothing) to which single would be their debut; from who would design their artwork (they weren't having any of our in-house crap) to what radios and TVs they could be arsed to get out of bed for.

Come November 1976, 'Anarchy in the UK' was ready for release. The single's promotional images were suitably iconoclastic. A Union Jack was torn to shreds, then reassembled with safety pins. 'An affront to the Establishment?' For fuck's sake, it was only a lark! I played the single to the Major General, my father-in-law, who pronounced it 'jolly good.' He wasn't in the least bit bothered by the butchered Union Jack. Only a bit of rag! Nothing like a touch of old-fashioned outrageousness to shake up the status quo, what? Famous last words.

19

ANARCHY IN THE UK

Punk Rock was now the greatest musical phenomenon since Merseybeat. I was slavering like a rabid pack dog on the hunt, to track down and sign up for their music publishing other artists of the genre now referred to as 'New Wave'. How the punks gobbed on that term: I was getting the hang of the lingo, at least. I saw the Clash, and practically press-ganged them into accepting a deal. That fell to bits about three fences in. I coerced the Jam into the studio to record us a few demos, but that failed to go anywhere either. Such losses were frustrating. Well, they weren't really 'losses', were they, as they hadn't been ours in the first place. But desperation was mounting. Punk was gathering momentum. It would have looked great for us to have a couple more gob-and-slash acts on our publishing roster, if only any were forthcoming.

To promote their new single, the Sex Pistols were slated to headline a nineteen-date tour entitled 'Anarchy'. This was effectively a punk revue. The Clash, the Buzzcocks and the Damned would co-star, along with special guests the Heartbreakers: an American band conjured from the disintegration of the New York Dolls. The release of 'Anarchy in the UK' was set for 26th November. Having been the first to sign them, to the publishing division, it was unbelievably irritating to watch the record company having all the fun launching them. I did feel left out, and couldn't help wishing that I worked for the label instead. EMI's promotions team were having a field day. Things got even better for them when a gift of an opportunity arose.

Queen had been scheduled to appear on Thames TV's *Today* show on 1st December. This was a live programme offering prime, tea-time exposure just after 6pm, when most of the nation were watching television over their fish fingers or beans on toast. But Freddie Mercury went down with toothache so unbearable that he was forced to seek emergency treatment. Queen had to pull out of their appearance. Record plugger Eric Hall decided to put the Sex Pistols on instead. It was a massive risk, but so was signing this lot in the first place. It was too late in the day for the show to find and book anybody else, so Hall got away with it. The fly in the ointment was bibulous Bill Grundy, the show's middle-aged presenter, who had never heard of the band and who had zero interest in interviewing them. His superiors insisted otherwise.

The band arrived at the studio with several of their 'Bromley contingent' supporters in tow, including Siouxsie Sioux sporting braces and make-up that gave her the look of a malevolent mime artist. All were plied with free booze in the Green Room prior to the show. Steve Jones knocked back a whole bottle of Blue Nun, which was asking for trouble. They all went into the studio, the girls included. Grundy goaded the group. The boys taunted him back. The presenter then said something provocative to Siouxsie, implying that he was up for 'meeting her after,' which provoked a barrel of F-words from the wine-fuelled Jones. We weren't allowed to say the F-word on television in those days. 999 was dialled. Questions were asked in the House. It was the scandal du jour, and the press had a field day. Were we dreaming? We couldn't have paid for publicity on such a scale. The Pistols were upgraded to assault rifles.

First the triumph, then the fall-out. The Anarchy tour became a fiasco. With local councils out in force to ban them, only six of the nineteen dates went ahead. The press were still all over them: every move they made, every syllable they uttered was shock-rock headline news. Some members of Her Britannic Majesty's press corps attempted to bribe them into behaving even more disgracefully. The ladies at EMI's plant in Middlesex went out on strike, refusing to press copies of the single. They claimed to have been offended by the band's revolting language, overlooking the fact that their own fell well short of respectable. The radio stations shoved their oars in, refusing to play the record. The papers turned on EMI. Cliff Richard was appalled. Mischievous Malcolm McLaren claimed falsely, in an effort to whip up even more publicity, that Cockney Rebel's Steve Harley had them thrown off the label. As if.

All a maelström in a mug, in the scheme. The band were whisked off to Holland at the beginning of 1977, where they were instructed to play a few lame gigs, do a couple of tame TVs and keep their ugly heads down. But as with everything the Sex Pistols touched or got involved in, the plan disintegrated into chaos. During their performance on the show *Disco Circus*, apparently for no reason, a dwarf was brought out on stage. The Jones boy couldn't help himself. He started hitting the poor little guy repeatedly on the head with his guitar neck. Up rocked the cavalry from EMI, inflamed to boiling point by exaggerated accounts of even worse behaviour of which the band weren't guilty, but which had been dreamed up down the pub by shameless British tabloid hacks. The label had had enough, and had come to inform the band that they were dumping them. This of course meant that we would lose their publishing too.

The Sex Pistols left EMI, not with a whimper but with a bang that would reverberate for years to come. Out went the upstarts and in came the original faces of teen rebellion: Ladies and Gentlemen, the Rolling STONES! Not even Ray Charles could have failed to see the irony. Mick Jagger couldn't resist a jibe at his new label's expense, announcing that, in the year of Her Majesty's Silver Jubilee, it 'felt right' to be signing to this esteemed establishment. He added that at least they weren't about to sack him for swearing on television. I am baffled to this day by the blind eyes that were turned to Keith Richards's string of drug offences around the world, while the Pistols failed miserably with a few F-words.

We thought *we'd* had a bad time. We'd got off lightly. The band's behaviour deteriorated spectacularly after they left us. Glen Matlock walked, unable to tolerate any longer the tension between him and Johnny. Rotten replaced him with his friend Simon Ritchie, re-invented as Sid Vicious. They signed to A&M, home of Yes and the Carpenters. 'We've only just begun' was the size of it. But their reign there lasted little more than a single night. Having drunk themselves titless in preparation for a photo opportunity to mark the deal, with Buckingham Palace of all places as the backdrop, they got into a fight in the limo en route, and had beaten each other half-way to St. George's Hospital by the time they arrived at the Monarch's primary residence. They then stormed the A&M offices and went berserk among the secretaries. Vicious soaked his bleeding foot in a Ladies' toilet while Jones had sex in the adjacent cubicle with a woman he'd only just met and may not even have known the name of. They were on a roll. Careening on down to The Speakeasy, they bumped into presenter 'Whispering Bob' Harris and threatened the throat out of him. Bob complained to A&M's head of A&R, Derek Green, who happened to be the guy who'd signed the Pistols. Green moaned to Malcolm McLaren, who expressed unrestrained delight. That was it. Enough. The rotters were sacked. 25,000 copies of their new single 'God Save The Queen' failed to make it as far as the shelves. The band moved on, to Richard Branson's Virgin.

I won't bore you with the rest. It's not why we're here. Besides, I was long off the case by then. I was merely another dismayed observer, along with the rest of the music industry, of the band's mindless self-destruction. Most music fans will have forgotten by now that they ever existed in the first place. Think 'Sex Pistols' today and the image that tends to surface, at least for those of us decrepit enough to remember, features the defiant faces of Glen's bass-playing replacement, Sid Vicious, and his dirty, pouty girlfriend, Nancy Spungen… she who was knifed to death in a bedroom in the Chelsea Hotel, New York. Sid was arrested for her murder and was released on bail. He was nicked again for attacking Patti Smith's brother in a club, and wound up on Rikers Island, where a heroin overdose did the rest.

Groups come, they go. Didn't I know it. Suffice it to say that the media and the band together did a comprehensive job of destroying the Sex Pistols. I was saddened by their demise. It affected me personally. I had been one of the first to perceive their potential. I was thrilled when we signed them for publishing. I watched from the wings in despair as hope and glory were slashed against the wall.

Plenty of damage was done, not least to EMI. The company took about a year to recover from the painfully public fall-out, the dent in their reputation and the widespread ridicule that ensued. One of the jokes doing the rounds of the music press held that the acronym EMI stood not for Electrical and Musical Industries but for Every Mistake Imaginable. The company went on to suffer one of the worst sales slumps in its history.

At the Christmas 1977 office party, I drank myself stupid alone in a corner, then did something so out of character that the thought of it still makes me cringe. I hit the dance floor. I forget now which Pistols single the DJ was spinning, but I threw myself into it as though the Reaper himself had come for me. After what felt like several hours but which was only about three minutes, the record faded. The dancing stopped. I glanced around. I was the only one out there on the dance floor. Every last guest had backed against the walls, like zombies melting silently into moonlight. All eyes were on me.

20

BIG MAC

EMI's publishing empire continued to expand. We acquired the Columbia Pictures music publishing groups, Colgems and Screen Gems. I had a Top Five hit in 1977 with the song 'Romeo', by a group I'd signed called Mr. Big. It couldn't have been more different from punk had it sabred its own throat. It had more in common with Bread and the Eagles than the anarchy touts. Which was fine by me.

As for my old chums Fleetwood Mac, 1977 was their year. Having relocated to California, Mick had met a loved-up couple recording as a duo called Buckingham Nicks. When guitarist Bob Welch left the band, Mick invited Lindsey Buckingham, an arrogant guitarist with a rep as a moody jerk, to take his place. Linds explained that he and Stevie came as a package. Mick obliged, the die was cast, and the blonde with a sound like Orson Welles on helium became the voice of big Mac. The restyled group enjoyed huge success with their first album together, 1975's *Fleetwood Mac*, which was the band's tenth album and their second eponymous LP (the first being their debut). This one, known as their 'White Album', possibly in homage to the Beatles, went to Number One on the US Billboard 200 a year after its release. It was the second-biggest album of 1976, boasting three Top Twenty singles – 'Over My Head', 'Rhiannon' and 'Say You Love Me' – and Stevie's exquisite 'Landslide', which she would go on to sing on virtually every FM tour. The follow-up album, recorded during the meltdown of the relationships of John and Christine McVie and Lindsey and Stevie, who were never married in the first place but might as well have been, transformed them into global superstars.

This excruciating, compelling, addictive multi-platinum soap opera was Music to Get Divorced By if ever there was. *Rumours* was the landmark, the moment of truth. Every track, from 'Dreams', 'Never Going Back Again' and 'Don't Stop' to 'The Chain' and 'Go Your Own Way' was a knife to the heart. It became their second Number One album in America, would go on to win the 1978 Grammy award for Album of the Year, and by March would have sold ten million copies.

Nothing for this band would ever be the same again. When they unpacked in London that April on their triumphant world tour, I trolled sheepishly along to the Rainbow and caught up with Mick backstage. So did Peter Green, though we managed to miss each other. How did that happen? What a reunion it would have been. I remember Mick's eyes glistening with mischief as he stood staring at me in his florist's shop that doubled as a dressing room. 'Dave!' he said expansively, throwing his leg-length arms as wide as the Thames. 'All this could have been *yours!*'

'You know me, Mick,' I smiled, 'the one who got away.'

I'd be lying if I said I didn't care. Fleetwood Mac were the biggest group in the world at that point. The quintessential rock superstars. They were buying mansions the way the rest of us buy books. I pictured them bathing in champagne, wafting about on clouds of coke, having mind-blowing sex with whoever took their fancy in Learjets and on the back seats of limousines. Their tangled love lives made A-list movie stars look like losers. They were more, much more than mere rock stars. They were gods and goddesses. They were living the dream. This was all so far removed from the quaint little plans Mick and I used to sit around making when we were teenagers, projecting ourselves into a rock'n'roll stratosphere that we doubted could really exist, that I burst out laughing. I nearly choked, I couldn't help myself. Did I regret walking away from Fleetwood Mac? Not especially. I knew myself too well by then. The stark truth was that I would never have survived what they had become. I would have gone for it, hell for leather, no holds barred. I would have drunk too much, drugged too much, fucked too much, died too much. I would have been the ultimate rock'n'roll suicide.

It looked easy from the outside. As an insider, I knew to my cost that it was anything but. In their shoes, I would have gasped my last on my way to the nearest body bag. Some are born to live their life in the limelight; to put up with the spleen-splitting drag of touring and performing, of having to create to order from scratch in the studio when you'd been sick to the stomach all night; of being deprived of any semblance of private life, of getting mobbed wherever you go, of needing security just to go for a piss; of that sinking feeling that everyone wants a piece of you, of never knowing for certain whether you've got a friend, or whether they love you for the money and the glory, and would no longer want to know you when your luck changed. Because it always changes, however long it takes. The crest of the wave must always come in to land. I reminded myself I was the lucky one. I may be a has-been; a never-was, more like. I may be living from wage packet to wage packet, on an income that would never cover the outgoings. Mick and his lovely Jenny had married, had a daughter, had affairs, got divorced. I had my beautiful wife and child, my friends were genuine, and I knew where I belonged. There were tears in my eyes as I hugged Mick goodbye. I wondered, as I walked the long way home, whether I'd ever see him again.

★

Back to reality. There were more near-misses than there were celebrated signings, but that was par for the course. At least the menu was varied. My remit was broad, from Paul McCartney's Frog Chorus song 'We All Stand Together' – as I told him, an absolutely abominable record – to Tom Robinson, whose '2-4-6-8 Motorway' and 'Glad to be Gay' were outstanding. The latter song was radical in its time. Tom was in some ways the herald of Frankie Goes to Hollywood and Erasure. I landed the Q-Tips, a blue-eyed soul and new wave rock band fronted by the pre-heartthrob Paul Young. They had a terrific fan base and were one of the best live groups on the circuit. They went on to support the Who on tour in 1981. And I bagged us new wave power popsters the Vapors, who had been discovered by the Jam's bass player Bruce Foxton, and whose 'Turning Japanese' has never gone away.

The late-Seventies post-punk landscape was as bleak as it got, but every now and then came a beacon to light our way. I signed the Gang of Four, a bunch of Leeds University neo-Marxists who seemed to take themselves rather too seriously. Were they communists? Who knew.

When they knocked back the vodka of an evening and threw their glasses into the fire, they'd laugh it off as a Bolshevik ritual. Were they the new Sex Pistols? Should I be running a mile? I wasn't quite sure what to do at that point, so I just nodded and ordered another round. Their funky, dance-y, reggae-infused debut album *Entertainment!* was released in 1979. I heard them described as a hybrid of the Sex Pistols and James Brown, which seemed about right. Whatever else they aspired to be, the songs were a vehicle for their socio-political philosophy. Their first single 'Damaged Goods' had been an indie chart hit on the Scottish Fast Product label. BBC Radio 1's John Peel championed it. Their appearance on his 'Sessions' show earned them a contract with EMI. Now that they were signed to the record label, we got them for publishing. Which confused me. Weren't we precisely the kind of evil capitalist corporate machine that they so despised? Could this be subversion from within? How were we going to get a hit out of them? We certainly needed one.

Promotion did what they did best. The single 'At Home He's a Tourist' made it far enough up the chart to warrant an appearance on *Top Of The Pops.* Then somebody made a complaint about their lyric reference to 'rubbers', as we once called condoms. This was deemed too risqué for a show watched by millions of kids. The band were asked to sing the word 'rubbish' instead. They grumbled, backed down, flared up again, calmed down, and eventually offered a milder alternative. This too was denounced as unacceptable. They lost their rag and stormed off the set.

Both single and album were reviewed favourably. The music press loved them. But the single was banned by both radio and television, and the record company started to lose interest in them. The band were never as big as they should have been, but their influence endured. It was infinitely more far-reaching than that of countless top-selling acts. Of this phenomenon, the Velvet Underground were another example. If not for the Gang of Four, perhaps no R.E.M., no Red Hot Chili Peppers. Kurt Cobain once said that Nirvana started out as a Gang of Four and Scratch Acid rip-off. The band were also beloved of many a rap metal outfit. Prestige acts are essential to the mix. They might not sell millions in their own right, but they often inspire those who do. Dump them from the roster and the food chain fails. They are a vital part of the culture.

★

My wife Angie miscarried our triplets and I hit an all-time low.

Why do things happen out of the blue? They probably don't. There is a rhythm to life, and always a reason. Not that I could work out what that was. The last group I'd played with before chucking rock'n'roll to reinvent myself a music publisher reared its head again. Co-band member Martin Glover and I found ourselves back in the studio. We revisited our old work. Tentatively at first, and then with mounting vigour. We emerged with greatly-improved, infinitely more polished recordings of the songs we had written in another life, about other times, which then somehow found their way to US label Monarch Records. You could have knocked me flying with a prawn cracker when they offered us a recording deal. What now? I lost sleep. Maybe my reunion with Mick Fleetwood backstage at the Rainbow in April had had something to do with it. Perhaps it had stirred some old ghosts, and reminded me of unfinished business. Or maybe I'd simply had it up to here with music publishing. The job was mostly mindless pen-pushing, nothing like the glamorous, expense-account-driven caper it had been cracked up to be. If I persevered at EMI, I would skulk forever in Terry Slater's shadow, flogging myself half to death and being deprived of credit, which he would always make sure he got. Making music was my passion, my life blood. I had convinced myself that I could live without it, but could I really? I figured I had one last chance, a last-ditch attempt. Now or never. But every time I plucked up the courage to tell Angie that this was what I wanted to do, reality yanked me back down to earth. The burden of responsibility weighed heavily. I was a father. It was what I had always wanted. We had another one on the way. After the tragedy of the triplets, it was huge blessing. EMI was our stability. This new record deal promised nothing at all, while threatening to destroy everything we had. It was a no-brainer.

I stayed on at EMI. Martin Glover and I parted company. The tapes of our magnum opus were consigned to a drawer, where they would sit gathering dust for the next forty years. I was never able to bring myself to throw them away. Nor could I ever force myself to listen to them. They were the siren calls of phantoms, the echoes of a band that never was. They were relevant only in my formless and chaotic dreams. It was only when I slept that I could hear them. The music business had moved on, I kept telling myself. Who on earth had the remotest interest in mellifluous choruses about queens, wizards and Marrakech squares in 1979? I galvanised myself. I put away childish things.

21

NEW ROMANTICS

One of our last signings of both the Seventies and to EMI Publishing started life as a punk group in Birmingham. They evolved into an eight-piece collective who specialised in Sixties R&B and soul covers: Aretha Franklin's 'Respect', Sam & Dave's 'Hold On, I'm Coming', that kind of thing. They changed their name from the Killjoys to Dexys Midnight Runners, and released their first record, 'Dance Stance' on the indie label Oddball Records. EMI acquired the licensing deal and the song went to Number Forty, buying them a slot on *Top Of The Pops*. There was a sense, from the off, that this band could go all the way. They had spirit, they thought big, and they reminded me of the music I'd once listened to in Soho's sweaty dungeons during the Sixties. Yet revivalists they were not. The press read them wrongly, and from that day forward the band's relationship with both nationals and music papers would be uneasy. Not that there was anything wrong with retro. The Jam were doing it too, spearheading Mod's second wave. Immersed in a grim, austerity-ridden present, more than a few artists and bands were choosing to revisit music of the past, and to repackage it for an optimistic future.

So Dexys were no nostalgia act. They were never quite convincing as that. This was thanks to quirky Kevin Rowland, who was both their frontman and their in-house Svengali. Some called their style fancy dress – jodhpurs and velvet one minute, donkey jackets and woolly hats the next – but there was something pavement-level and wonderfully appealing about it. It was clear from the start that Rowland called the shots. He banned his band from drinking and taking drugs. He forced them to rehearse obsessively. He shouted them into submission. Not a collective at all, then. More like a dictatorship. It occurred to me early on that Kevin was not quite stable. Well. Show me a rock star who is. I had infinite experience of this phenomenon. I'd even suffered from it myself. I was more than equipped to take this mug on. I loved the band's sound, and I was prepared to put the hours in. Let's see what we could make of this little lot.

Kevin's odd singing voice didn't come naturally. It took time to grow. It was a while before that wobbly warble emerged. I heard it catch between his tonsils one day. I felt it as it started start to vibrate. I knew he was onto something.

Only three of Dexys members, the so-called 'nucleus', fell under the EMI deal. It was a strange way to do music business, and was therefore destined to breed ill-feeling within the group. Again, this could not be called collectivism. The publishing deal was better, however, ensuring that each specific songwriter would receive his own royalties. But overall, the arrangement was messy, and ultimately doomed.

Kevin was adamant that 'Geno' should be their first single. EMI Records disagreed. I thought that they should go with it, and was relieved when the record company capitulated, because it had been one of the songs that convinced me to sign them for publishing. The song was about Geno Washington, for whom Shotgun Express had opened, all those years ago. This tribute with a twist captured his magic. I knew in my bones that it would be a hit. My little daughter loved it. During the early months of the new decade, it was, of course, a chart-topper. Things then went horribly wrong. Which I had seen coming.

Dexys were despatched to Oxford's Chipping Norton studios to record their debut album. Producer Pete Wingfield had been selected partly because the group liked his single 'Eighteen with a Bullet', partly because he'd played in Geno Washington's band during the early Seventies, and partly because Van Morrison had been offered the job but had stalked out of the rehearsal before they recorded a note. Things proceeded smoothly with Pete until recording had concluded. But when the producer left the studio, a couple of the group leapt up to restrain the engineer while the others made off with the master tapes. They legged it up the A40 with the police in hot pursuit. You couldn't make it up. EMI had done it again, saddling themselves with another treacherous act. Dexys held the label to ransom, demanding a better royalty rate. EMI gave in, and the tapes were surrendered. This was done via the London underground, risking magnetic damage to the analogue tapes. Looks like they made it.

Against all odds, their album *Searching For the Young Soul Rebels* was released in July 1980. The music press loved it, and it became a Top Ten hit. But EMI couldn't forgive them for their appalling behaviour. They'd only just begun, but their days were numbered.

★

Terry Slater and I went up in the world. For whatever reason, undoubtedly a spurious one, we were uprooted from boring old music publishing and replanted in Artists and Repertoire. What on earth did either of us know about *that*? Who cared, we'd give it our best shot. At long last I'd be going to work every day at EMI HQ in Manchester Square, where I would be responsible for every single aspect of my artists' careers. Not only would I be a bona fide A&R man, out there scouting for artists to sign to the record label, but I would also be involved in the selection of producers, and would even get to oversee the recording process. It was a massive step up. I wasn't sure quite what I'd done to deserve it, but I kept my mouth shut and got on with it.

To the outside world, it appeared as though I was suddenly responsible for steering the careers of the label's most sensational and world-beating acts: Paul McCartney, Queen, Pink Floyd, Kate Bush and so on. It wasn't quite like that. Such artists preceded me by some considerable time. Queen, for example, had been part of the stable since their early management and recording masterminds Trident had signed Queen's first contract with EMI in 1973. Their debut, eponymous album was released that July. By the time I arrived, they had already reached the stage in their career at which they were calling their own shots, and didn't need me or anybody else to look after them. It was not for me to tell them which track should be the next single or where they should be looking to shoot their next video. Their lawyer-manager Jim Beach, who oversees them to this day, would simply march onto the premises and say, *this* is the next single, *this* is where the tour will be going, and so on, and we would have to accept what we were told. So I never had much work to do as far as Queen were concerned. It was what you might call an arm's-length relationship. I was only there to make sure that nothing went wrong. Not that anything ever did go wrong, with them. They were supremely professional and in control. I did get to go, at the band's invitation, to some utterly wonderful parties. Although I met Brian May, Roger Taylor and John Deacon many times, I never once met Freddie Mercury. To my knowledge, he had never visited EMI. I didn't even get to meet him at their after-show party at the Roof Gardens in 1986, which both authors of this book attended. It was all a bit much, actually. Even for me. I remember lurking in the shadows, feeling out of place and overwhelmed. Perhaps it was the sight of the naked bellhops, lift attendants and waiting staff, all of whom were completely stark-naked, their bodies painted to look as though they were wearing uniforms or chunks of forest.

As for Pink Floyd, the quintessential prog rockers had been with the company since 1967, the year they signed for the mind-boggling advance of £5,000 – the best part of a hundred grand today – and when their first single, 'Arnold Layne', was released on the Columbia label. It hadn't all been plain sailing: their debut was banned by a number of radio stations because of its references to cross-dressing, an outrage back then. A certain amount of jiggery pokery on the part of the record retailers ensured the record's ascent to a respectable Number Twenty. Their follow-up, 'See Emily Play', did much better, and climbed to the Number Six slot. Some high-profile TV appearances followed, during which it became apparent that their gorgeous, gifted and ethereal frontman Syd Barrett was coming off the rails. LSD was most likely to blame. By the time EMI-Columbia released the band's first album, *The Piper at the Gates of Dawn*, in August that year, Barrett was in the throes of full mental breakdown. It was up hill and down dale from then on. All too soon, Barrett's tragedy would be compounded when he was replaced by Dave Gilmour. Syd forged on with his band as a 'non-performing songwriter'. For a while, at least. But come the following year, he was out. Looking back, there are parallels to be drawn with the life and demise of dear Peter Green. Syd left the planet in July 2006, God bless him. Things could have turned out very differently had I accepted an invitation to become Pink Floyd's co-manager. Steve O'Rourke, who assumed control of their team in 1968 and remained at the helm until his death in 2003, implored me early on to join him. I turned him down: I had a good thing going at EMI. It was flattering to be asked, but no regrets.

★

1980 stands out in my mind as an odd year. Hits like Dexys 'Geno' aside, record sales slumped. Our successful sellers were primarily by the big-name acts: Paul McCartney's *McCartney II* and Kate Bush's *Never For Ever*: the first Number One studio album by a British female artist. It was co-produced by Kate, which didn't surprise me. She had been composing and recording from an early age, and certainly knew her way around a studio. By the time she was sixteen, she had been turned down by several record labels. Then she happened to meet David Gilmour through a friend of her brother's. He recognised her magic, got involved, and brought her to his own record company. In 1978, when she was still only nineteen, she celebrated her first Number One with her debut single release, 'Wuthering Heights'. It made her the first-ever female artist to score a chart-topper with a self-penned song. *Never For Ever* was classic Kate, who had always been a law unto herself. It also featured the Fairlight sampling synthesizer. EMI promoted the album with cinematic videos. For all her apparent hippy-dippiness, their favourite daughter was maturing into a truly compelling artist.

The music industry was evolving, and music journalism was forced to change too, in order to keep pace. As interest in traditional weeklies declined, along came a vibrant new magazine to spice things up. Originally launched in October 1978, *Smash Hits* had been slow to pick up but was now a force to be reckoned with. Glossy and colourful, packed with photos, trivia and, crucially, song lyrics, it marked a turning point.

★

I had thought that I'd seen the back of Malcolm McLaren. The flame-haired poison dwarf turned up like a bad penny, radioactive in an electric blue suit. With that shock of orange hair flaring out of his head, he looked like a Roman candle. What did *he* want? He was flogging a new band. Of course he was. He called his latest effort Bow

Wow Wow.

Malcolm had been in Paris for the past few years, making soundtracks for porn flicks. On his return to London, he'd got friendly with a regular visitor to the King's Road Sex shop: the artist formerly known as Stuart Goddard. Young Stu had reinvented himself as Adam Ant. Malcolm stole his band and dumped Adam. Ant just thumbed his nose and went off to reinvent swashbuckling romanticism with a Burundi beat. The latter element had been Malcolm's idea. Touché.

Bow Wow Wow were also deploying the Burundi beat, but what the hell. You can never have too much of a good thing. Annabella Lwin, this new band's singer, was only fourteen years old. Which was suspect. According to McLaren, he had handpicked this angel because she looked the part: a prepubescent girl snatched by a pirate from a Mauritian island. 'Real jailbait stuff,' Malcolm gloated. The myth was that he'd spotted her in a launderette, but he made that up. It was all a bit kinky for my taste. Piracy was clearly the theme, in more ways than one. Their first single 'C-30 C-60 C-90 Go' was a shameless celebration of home taping: the practice that, we were now informing fans via a record-sleeve campaign, was 'killing music'. In a year when music sales were at an all-time low, it was clear that McLaren was still on a mission to destroy the industry from within. When the band and the deal fell apart, he ordered his charges to the EMI offices and commanded them to smash the place up. Yet again, a Malcolm McLaren-fuelled act of vandalism heaped chaos on EMI.

★

Dexys weren't the only band out of Birmingham to cross my path. A caller by the name of Paul Berrow got through to me on the phone one day to chat about his charges Duran Duran. They were named, he said, after the evil scientist in Jane Fonda's late Sixties Sci-Fi film *Barbarella*. He invited me to come and check them out at a venue called Holy City Zoo. I received more such invitations each week than I could ever have scoffed hot dinners. I couldn't possibly jump at them all. But there was something about that name that piqued my interest. I could see it now, on magazine covers and record sleeves. Could I hear them in my mind's ear on the radio? I would soon find out.

I went to their gig in Birmingham, and found myself thrilled by them. They were still rough around the edges and their playing was somewhat scratchy, but the panache, the attitude and the ideas were great. It would be a doddle to slick them up. They had extraordinary presence, much as the Pistols had had, but they were a lot less confrontational, and far more 'showbiz'. I just knew, there and then, that these guys would be massive. After the glory of punk, its intimidation, rough chords and attitude, I sensed that the next generation needed something completely different.

My thought processes were working on a social as well as on a musical/entertainment plane. These artists were of a high standard. Guitarist Andy Taylor knew a hell of a lot of chords. He reminded me of George Harrison in the early days of the Beatles. As for Simon Le Bon, the singer – real name – he had star quality scrawled all over him. It struck me that he had the potential to go all the way as a kind of 1980s Elvis. The songs were brash, blatant and catchy, a bunch of advert jingles with groove. This was music that bored into your brain and took up residence behind your eardrums. I couldn't get it out of my head, one song in particular: 'Girls on Film'. I could hear them on the radio, all right. On every station in every nation, 24/7. I had no choice but to sign them. In some ways, it was as if they were signing *me*.

What would Terry say? I couldn't wait to get back to London to tell him all about them. He trusted my judgement by now, I could tell, because no sooner had I mentioned them than he was jumping around, talking about a deal. Off I trotted to see the group again, this time in Leeds, and met the boys after the show. Negotiations with Berrow led to an opportunity for me to accompany the band on tour, travelling with them in a cramped Winnebago truck as they wended their way around the UK in support of Hazel O'Connor.

I liked these guys. They were friendly and polite, and eager to please. There was nothing arrogant about them, they were down to earth. Just as easy on the eye as Simon were the bassist John Taylor and the keyboard player, Nick Rhodes. Drummer Roger Taylor could have been a matinée idol posing as a thumper. Guitarist Andy Taylor, looking like the shy boy next-door but never playing like it, completed the line-up. These Taylors were not related, which would make for good copy. Their managers, however, were brothers. Paul and Michael Berrow obviously knew what they were doing. The savvy sometime-club owners had built this group from scratch, assembling an impressive package with an eye on the primary prize: a recording contract with one of the majors. They wanted a label who demanded hits. They had come to the right place.

Simon Le Bon from Bushey turned out to have been the final piece of the Duran Duran jigsaw that had taken a while to create. He'd been a choir boy, and had the requisite angelic look – of one who'd been caught behind the choir stalls with a girlie mag. He had fronted a post-punk outfit called Dog Days. He'd been a child actor, if you could call it acting, in a television advert for washing powder. His mother and grandmother had been dancers; something in him sought to follow in their dainty footsteps. He admired the moody, electronic music this new group were making. He knew that he could interpret it, and give it swank.

While every one of them looked the part, they didn't strike me as posers. They were grafters too, and had a game plan. They had set their sights on London's Hammersmith Odeon in 1982, Wembley Arena in 1983, and New York's Madison Square Garden in 1985. They didn't want much. Neither did we.

By the time they came to my attention, they were already on their way. They had become a local sensation in Birmingham as the house band of the Berrow brothers' Rum Runner club. They had recorded demos at London's AIR studios, and they had performed at the Marquee Club. They'd supported some unlikely headliners, and were now ready to strike out in their own right. They wanted to be the band playing 'when the bomb drops', 'when the Titanic hits the iceberg'. Oh yes, they were already speaking in headlines. They wanted to face the music, dance, and smother the pages of *Jackie* magazine and *Smash Hits*. They wanted to be splashed all over the national newspapers. I could see it all coming.

By the early Eighties, image had become an essential part of pop stardom. Clothes, make-up, style and stance were now every bit as important as catchy songs. The pioneer of Glam, Marc Bolan, was dead, killed in a car crash just before his thirtieth birthday in September 1977. But his legacy, in terms of style and attitude as a means to embellish music, lived on. From the point of view of image alone, the Durans couldn't fail. They were modern dandies who loved dressing up. They seemed tailor-made for the new wave of style glossies

– *i-D*, *The Face*, *Blitz* – all of which majored on pop's relationship with fashion. *Top Of The Pops*, now dowdy and on the downslide into middle age, was taking an interest in its appearance again, as though it were having an affair. Even two-toners Madness staged striking performances in which Ska met music hall, with clothes to match. I'd considered signing them to EMI Publishing a while back, but had foolishly ignored the advice of my wife Angie. I should have listened. She was right, they *were* going to be huge. Reader, I passed.

Adam Ant got his revenge on Malcolm McLaren at last, by becoming a massive pop star. His eccentric look – highwayman meets pirate meets warpainted Apache – displayed a savvy that rivalled that of his dastardly former manager. With hits like 'Stand and Deliver', 'Antmusic' and 'Prince Charming', he beat the chancer at his own game and buried Bow Wow Wow. *Next.*

The New Romantics were now the dominant musical genre. You didn't have to go far to find them. The more elite London clubs were heaving with them, particularly the Blitz: a Tuesday-nighter, where George O'Dowd manned the cloakroom before reinventing himself as Boy George; where the clubbers rocked up in fancy dress and panto wear, oh yes they did, and got turned away at the door if they didn't look over-the-top enough; and where Islington boys Spandau Ballet were the house band. The rivalry between them and the Durannies had already kicked off, across the music pages at least. I tried to sign the Spands too, but they went with Chrysalis Records. I fobbed off my failure to bag them by pretending that their manager Steve Dagger had demanded too great a wardrobe budget. The amazing thing about that period was that virtually everyone on the scene had the potential to become a star. Even the Blitz Club's host had made a record. After appearing in the video for David Bowie's 'Ashes to Ashes', Steve Strange recorded 'Fade to Grey' as part of Visage. The New Romantics, in a nutshell, were about future nostalgia. But they weren't out of nowhere. They were doing what pop had always done, fashioning something old into something new. It was only spit and polish. Could this be a sign that London was starting to swing again? I wouldn't go that far.

It occurred to me around this time that I brought something to the table that most other A&R men could not. I was a musician in my own right. I knew my way around a bass guitar, and other instruments too.

I knew about songwriting, arranging and producing, having done all of those things myself. I'd played in bands with a string of household names. I spoke the language of the artists and acts I was now working with. I understood their creative angst. I wasn't just another corporate bean-counter.

★

Duran Duran came in some pomp and circumstance to visit EMI's HQ. It wasn't just the chiefs eager to sign them who hurried down to pay homage. Secretaries from all over the building gathered to admire them. They stood around in small groups, smiling and swooning at the pretty boys all the way from sunny Birmingham. As the band undulated across our floor as if walking out on stage in front of thirty thousand fans, Terry Slater drew himself to his full height and made himself known. He shook hands all round and repeated his name effusively. My heart sank as he started on his usual spiel. I paced the room. I'd done so much to win this group. They were mine. Their relationship was with *me*. I wasn't going to let bloody Slater swoop in again and steal all the glory.

I got my wish. By the end of the year, the band had signed a contract with EMI. It was a smartly-negotiated deal. They asked for a very modest advance and weekly retainers, but good royalties. They knew they were going to be big. They shared the royalties equally among all their members. They were a team, a gang, and they were in it together. They were ready to conquer the world.

The year ended with triumph and tragedy. John Lennon was shot and killed outside his New York apartment by a deranged fan, and a light went out in the world. His death cast a shadow over those exuberant last days of 1980, not least through the corridors of EMI. The death of a former Beatle was like the loss of a family member. Christmas was cancelled. Kate Bush's new single, as bad luck would have it, was 'December Will Be Magic Again'. Only it wasn't, was it. It was anything but. The bad news broke and the record stalled, languishing just outside the Top Thirty.

But there was magic behind closed doors. Angie gave birth for the second time, and presented me with our firstborn son. We had a boy child for Christmas, and we were beyond ecstatic. Where there's life, there is hope.

22

HUNGRY LIKE THE FUCKIN' WOLF

I had begun pondering what the debut Duran Duran single should be before the ink was even dry on the contract. We were up against it now, because Spandau Ballet had already released their debut, 'To Cut a Long Story Short'. It had zipped to Number Five, and all eyes were on them. We had one chance to get both the first single and album right, and the responsibility was mine. I mustn't fuck it up. The buck stopped with the A&R guy. If we failed, it would be all my fault. The first thing I had to do was find the right producer. We kicked around a few ideas and spent many hours on the phone seeking advice from those who knew best. We weighed up our options, then I returned to my original hunch. We went with Colin Thurston.

Colin was frighteningly talented, and had an impressive CV. Boiled down, he'd worked with many of the Durans' primary influences, including David Bowie, whose "Heroes" album he had co-engineered in Berlin. He had also co-produced Lust for Life, Bowie's second album with Iggy Pop. He was amenable, collaborative, a coaxer. He was patient. He believed in taking his time to get things right. He was also an incredibly sweet person, and I knew the band would love him. His engineering background enabled him to capture the contribution of each individual musician. This was a balancing act as well as a science especially when orchestrating so many different styles.

The initial recording sessions took place in London before the band decamped to Chipping Norton studios, scene of the Dexys Midnight Runners tape-stealing scandal. There were a few hurdles to overcome, not least Simon's initial inability to adjust from stage to studio. But things soon ironed out. I wasn't worried. When I heard the final mixes, I was ecstatic. Colin had brought out the best in them, as I knew he would. Simon's voice sounded incredible. He brought far more presence to these finished recordings than he had to any of the demos. Colin had pulled off the most brilliant coup, and had captured the band with majesty. Now it was the turn of Marketing. Perry Haines, editor of style magazine *i-D*, took the band shopping for New Romantic clobber. He also kindled an interest in Bryan Ferry's favourite designer, Antony Price. Photographer Andy Earl set up sessions in Milton Keynes, at which both excelled. Posing and posturing came as naturally to the boys as playing music. After much deliberation, we went with 'Planet Earth' as the first single. Its vaguely Sci-Fi flavour was only a vehicle for the song's themes: the urgency of youth, a band desperate to be heard, the realisation of pop's ultimate dream. It was synth-driven and of the moment, and it was perfect. With the clubs in mind, they'd cut night versions of this and several other tracks, which were extended for the dancefloor. These were not mere remixes but played live, stretching out each song's grooves to maximise its dance-ability. 'Girls on Film' received a string-soaked treatment reminiscent of Studio 54, but 'Planet Earth' was the stand-out.

The perfect pop song required wrapping to match. Sleeve design was and remains a vital component of an artist's branding. The creation of a strong visual identity and the use of advertising parlance were no longer to be sniffed at. Not in Duran Duran's world, at least. They were more than up for screaming it from the rooftops, whatever it took. The artwork we commissioned was exceptional. The new red logo announced their name as if they were an airline or a fizzy drink. The message being that this was a *brand*, not merely a band. You didn't just listen to Duran Duran: you lived, breathed, danced to, ate to, did your homework to and argued with your mum to them. You slept beneath pictures of them plastered to your bedroom walls. Let them in and they would invade and dominate your entire life.

The radio stations went mad for 'Planet Earth'. A new entry out of nowhere at Number Twenty-Six, it took a few people by surprise. DJ Tony Blackburn mispronounced their name live on air, and the gaffe would follow them (and him) around for years. They landed their spot on *Top Of The Pops* in timely fashion. The show itself had a new producer and had undergone a complete transformation, as if in their honour. The boys rose to the occasion, and they smashed it. They mimed the song, of course, because this that was the way it was done in those days . There was a lot wrong with the presentation, but somehow it worked. The single marched on, peaking at Number Twelve. They'd gone in guns blazing, and they had done me proud. Thanks to a superb promo video directed by Russell Mulcahy, the record went all the way in Australia.

Timing is everything. 1981 was the year of the synthesizer, and few recordings remained untouched. I remember in particular 'Tainted Love' by Soft Cell, the Human League's 'Dare', 'New Life' by Depeche Mode, 'Only You' by Yazoo. Japan scored a Top Ten hit with 'Ghosts'. Duran Duran were nothing if not part of the zeitgeist. Electronics were only one aspect of their multi-layered sound, mind. They had more than enough going for them to convince fans that they were not just another fad. Many artists out-sold them that first year, it must be said, but the band weren't bothered. It wasn't just about chart positions. They were focusing all the way to stadium gigs and global superstardom.

Alas, their follow-up was spectacularly misjudged. I admit, it was all our fault. We insisted on 'Careless Memories' as the second single. We had even shot a video, which with hindsight was truly naff. The record flopped. It was no excuse that video promotion was still in its infancy, because the problem was the content: it was completely at odds with the music. However this had occurred, it must not be allowed to happen again. It never did. One failure was enough for the band to insist on having a say in their singles releases. The record stalled at Number Thirty-Seven. I took myself off to the pub and licked my wounds. The single should have done a better job of preparing the way for the album. We needed to be selling shedloads of singles in order for their album to be a success. But it wasn't just about them: my own job depended on it. The band were sympathetic about that. They themselves defended the record. They had a soft spot for it. Going forward, they would often close their shows with it. But for now, it had let them down.

The self-titled album came out in June, and surpassed all expectations. It reached Number Three, and stayed in the UK Top 100 for a hundred and eighteen weeks. By December the following year it would go platinum. But while its commercial success surpassed expectation, the critical response was dry. Granted, there were a few rave reviews by significant journalists, but these were drowned out by a chorus of vitriol. The *NME* seemed to despise them on principle. Their vicious denunciation was out of all proportion to the crime. *Smash Hits* didn't go a bundle on them either. One writer in particular, Neil Tennant, damned their image with faint praise, and bemoaned the lack of numbers in their repertoire.

I was baffled by all this. I took it personally. It felt like criticism for the sake of it, garnished with envy and resentment. This band were going places. The pinball wizard could have told you that. For this, they were sneered at. It's worth noting how many music writers happen to be failed or aspiring musicians. Perhaps they thought Duran Duran had helped themselves to limelight that was rightfully theirs. Perhaps it was because the band oozed sex, all the way from the bass lines and drum beat to Simon's pouting, pillowy lips. Girls wanted these boys. This was more than evident on their Faster Than Light tour, which confirmed them as the latest teen sensation. The next single, 'Girls on Film', clinched the deal. The sexy video featuring Sumo wrestlers and barely-clad models was banned. Marvellous! It looks ridiculously tame now – check it out – but oh, how it shocked the world back then. The record climbed to Number Five, their biggest hit to date. I went to the States to sell the band to EMI's American arm, Capitol Records. I got short shrift. According to them, disco was deceased. Idiots. It wasn't dead, it was anything but. It was moving with the times. Everyone was doing it: Diana Ross, Michael Jackson, Blondie. In any case, Duran Duran weren't disco. That genre was certainly one of their influences, but they were hardly slaves to its beat. It occurred to me that 'The Suits' didn't get it because the Durans could not be categorised. They hadn't the foggiest as to which radio stations they should play them on.

I badgered them. They backed down. They gave it a go. *Duran Duran* was duly released on Capitol's Harvest imprint. Its reception was predictably lukewarm. We knew that 'breaking the band in the States' was an integral part of their master plan. If we, their record company, hadn't achieved this by the time their contract came up for renewal, we feared that we would lose them to one of our rivals. I knew, and I told them, that the only way to succeed was to go for it live. Plus, as good luck would have it, the MTV music television network had just launched. They would soon be crying out for content of the banned 'Girls on Film' video variety. So we mounted them an American tour, and got them a meeting with MTV in New York. They sorted out their own first encounter with Andy Warhol. He fell in love with them. Coming face to face with Nick Rhodes for the first time must have been, for the shock-haired artist, like staring in the mirror at his nineteen year-old self. They hung out with him, talked music and art with him, went clubbing with him. He lavished attention on them. He took them to Studio 54. His diaries heaved with entries about my boys over the years, including an admission that he wanked to their videos. What more could they ask for? What more could *I* ask for? I was now EMI A&R's bright young star. This time, I made sure I was right at the front in the photograph. Though there wasn't much I could do to stop Terry Slater from muscling in too.

The time had come for the all-important second album. Recorded with Colin again at George Martin's AIR Studios above Oxford Circus, *Rio* was a masterclass in sonic experimentation. Not only were the songs brilliant, but both band and producer surpassed themselves. The perfect balance that they achieved on their debut was even more heightened. From the title track to 'Save A Prayer' to 'Hungry Like The Wolf', the album exploded with confidence. They'd honed a commercial, classy sound that I believed couldn't fail. I was well aware that bassist John Taylor was doing a legion's supply of marching powder, and I was concerned. What if it got the better of his ability, I fretted. Unable to fault his musicianship, I turned a blind eye. The band's sound had become, quite literally, Roxy Music on drugs. Keep this up and they were most definitely heading for Madison Square Garden. I allowed myself a brief pause from the fray, to relish the perfect moment and to breathe a sigh of relief. By monumental effort, determination and some intangible sweet alchemy, it had come together. Duran Duran were about to be bigger than they themselves could have imagined. Never again would things be so harmonious.

No sooner had they completed the album than the entire band minus Nick took a flight to Sri Lanka. Rhodes stayed behind with Colin to refine the mixes. Only when both were completely satisfied did Nick disappear to catch up with his friends. Someone at MTV had suggested Bond-style travelogues as perfect visual content for their burgeoning new channel. Duran Duran would be perfect for this, wouldn't they? Off they went to make travelogues with Russell Mulcahy. EMI would fund the £30,000 shoot provided the band agreed to shoot short feature films that we could use as videos. That sounds like a meagre budget today, but back then it was *huge*. The results, for 'Hungry Like The Wolf' and 'Save A Prayer', were astonishing. Not quite as astonishing as the one they shot on a yacht in Antigua for 'Rio', dressed incongruously in bright Antony Price suits. These videos would earn them even more vilification from the critics who had despised them in the first place, and who now regarded them as the personification of Thatcherite greed. What the hell, they were colourful. For every disparager there were a thousand Duran posters on teenage bedroom walls. It irritated the life out of me that the same writers who sat around lavishing Roxy Music's *Avalon* with carefully-couched praise were pouring scorn and spite all over 'Rio'. Show me the difference, assholes.

Duran's rivals Spandau Ballet had switched up their sound with their new release, 'Chant No. 1'. Boy George and Culture Club struck gold with their third single, 'Do You Really Want to Hurt Me?' ABC were also chasing our boys with an exceptional new Philadelphia-driven album, *The Lexicon of Love*. This one narked me, I have to say, as I'd tried to sign ABC myself. I'd gone all the way to Sheffield to knock on the front door of a squat. I needn't have bothered. I lost them to Phonogram. You win some, you lose some.

London was swinging, in spite of rising unemployment. 'Rio' was out, and *Smash Hits* gave them a rave review. We were winning them round at last. The singles went stellar. 'Hungry Like The Wolf' soared to Number Five. 'Save A Prayer', like the album, narrowly missed the top slot, and 'Rio' the single scored us a Number Nine. Michael Jackson called Nick to discuss a collaboration. It never happened, in the end, but how good was that?

Elsewhere, there were problems. Kate Bush's eccentric self-produced album *The Dreaming* failed to produce hit singles other than the track that had preceded the album's release, 'Sat In Your Lap'. She did make Number Three with the album, but feathers were ruffled all round. This was the closest EMI had come to rejecting a record. Why did it fail? The content was superlative, but its commercial potential was negligible. Her challenging songs shone a light on the dark side of ambition. Had she lost the plot? The punters didn't want all that. They wanted 'Eye Of The Tiger' and 'Fame'. They wanted hope. They wanted escapism. They wanted Duran Duran. Perhaps they even wanted the act I was about to sign: Kajagoogoo.

23

IS THERE SOMETHING
I SHOULD KNOW?

I had the Midas touch, apparently. Whatever I touched turned to Hit. Me, Dave Ambrose, the stereotypical acid-fried hippy. Trust me, there were plenty in the business who thought they were hearing things; who couldn't imagine me doing anything more business-like than frying onions on a hotdog stall outside Wembley Stadium. Not that I cared what they thought. I had never been one to sit around worrying about my reputation. Nor did I rest on my laurels. I knew better than anybody that the A&R man is only as good as his last hit, and that he is only ever one miss away from oblivion. Life moves very rapidly in rock and pop. The moment the hits dry up, the good is forgotten. Things moved even faster during the 1980s. We were on a fast-forward to annihilation, unless we kept a step ahead of everyone else.

It was thanks to Duran Duran that I found my next big artist. Hanging out at the Embassy Club on Bond Street one night, Nick Rhodes befriended a super-coiffed former waiter by the name of Christopher Hamill. Turning the letters of his surname around, the lad restyled himself 'Limahl'. The Embassy was London's answer to Studio 54. Its busboys wore tight, shiny shorts just as they did at the New York club. Swan down its elegantly-curved staircase and you found yourself immediately on the dance floor. Mick Jagger, Boy George, Frank Allen of the Searchers and countless other artists were regulars. Nick's new friend told him about his group Kajagoogoo. Nick came and told me. The next thing I knew, there they were, perched in my office. I signed them in July 1982. Such was the influence of Duran Duran that I was now signing bands I had previously seen fit to reject. I'd said no to these chancers before, as it happens. I chose not to remember.

Perhaps my own judgement, as well as timing, had a little to do with the change of heart. This group now seemed of the moment. Nick oversaw the production of their *White Feathers* album, collaborating again with Colin Thurston. I was very pleased. One song, 'Too Shy', stood out as the obvious first single. Its sultry mid-tempo verses reminding me of the kind of thing Leee John's group Imagination were doing. Its chorus might have been the most insanely infectious that I'd ever heard. The record shot to Number One early in 1983. When it cleaned up all over the world, I was not in the least surprised.

The follow-up, 'Ooh to be Aah', was another boppy one. We prepared ourselves to get cackling all the way down to Coutt's. We were not yet aware of the simmering divisions and rivalry within the band, nor of the fall-out that would follow. Limahl quit, and the band continued without him. Their similarly-coiffed bassist, former dustman Nick Beggs, now became their focal point. I must confess, I did miss Limahl. I wonder whatever happened to him? I guess he rose without trace. The band's 1984 single 'Big Apple' did go Top Ten, but then the album flagged. You can't always get what you want.

Another band that got away was Iron Maiden. According to their manager Rod Smallwood, I offered them a publishing deal after listening to a compilation album of new metal rock put together by Ashley Goodall, who had recently joined the staff at EMI. One of the tracks was 'Run to the Hills', from the band's forthcoming album *The Number Of The Beast*, about which there was quite a buzz. They declined my offer in favour of a superior one from Zomba.

Ashley Goodall also brought us Talk Talk. I assumed responsibility for them and all of their albums when Ashley left the company. I ran into trouble when I found myself down by some £250,000 on recording and general costs. We had reached the point of no return. That's when bands tend to get dropped. I didn't want that to happen to these guys, because I really believed in them. Executive David Munns, who would rise to become vice-chairman of the company, could see how much I loved this band. He accompanied me to see their producer, the magnificently-named Tim Friese-Greene, in 1984.

'Look,' we said, 'we've just got to have a hit single, or it's curtains.' They got the point, and they delivered us 'It's My Life'. *Bingo*. We then re-issued the first single, 'Talk Talk', which had originally been released two years earlier. 'Life's What You Make It' and 'Living In Another World' came later, in 1985 and 1986. But their relationship with their record company, which had never been that happy, soon soured. They sued EMI in the end. It happens.

★

Duran Duran's album *Rio* failed to set America alight. Until, that is, the meddlers at Capitol Records in the US had it remixed. What can you do? The boys knew that they were powerless to protest. Five songs were butchered, and were then reissued as an EP. It did the job. Or was MTV's high rotation of their video the move that clinched it? By March 1983, 'Hungry Like The Wolf' was Number Three on the Billboard chart, eclipsing its success back home. At last, there was no stopping them. A video-signing drew so many thousands of teenage girls to New York's Times Square that the ensuing pandemonium made headlines.

How did it feel to be a hit-maker? Reader, I was bemused. Now that my name was indelibly linked to the Durans, news of my connection to them leaked beyond the industry. Wannabe pop stars started tracking me down, following me about, and showering me with unwanted attention. Some went too far in their quest to get me to take notice of them. One even took off his trousers for me. Did I *look* like that kind of record company executive? My wife Angie reassured me that I did not.

Duran Duran's next single 'Is There Something I Should Know?' broke with tradition by being the work of an alternative producer. They enlisted the services of Ian Little, a production assistant on Roxy Music's *Avalon*. They were now going all-out to conquer US radio, eschewing nuance for the pummelling simplicity that appeared to be the American preference. The video, also a departure, was an exercise in restraint compared to its predecessors. There was nothing subtle or graceful about this new-sound, new-look Duran Duran. It worked.

As for their next album, they intended, they said, to record it with producer Alex Sadkin, he of Robert Palmer and Grace Jones fame, at his home studio: on Compass Point in Nassau, the Bahamas. Oh, *did* they, indeed. It would be great to get away from the relentless British press attention they said: look, the bastard tabloid paparazzi won't leave us alone, they're tailing us everywhere. Recording in the lap of luxury in exotic locations had become the latest trend in the music business, especially where tax advantages were to be had. But the question of budget was only ever a hangover away. It perturbed me. I was unable to sanction the Compass Point caper, so the band decamped to a huge chateau outside Cannes instead, to work on their album there. I use the term 'work' loosely, for nothing seemed to come of it.

They relocated to Montserrat. AIR Studios had created an impressive facility there. The Police (or 'Police', as they insisted on being called at the time), had recorded *Synchronicity* there. If it was good enough for them… But the Montserrat sessions, while more productive than those in France, were beset from the start with problems. The band whined endlessly about the set-up and the facilities. Nick had to be airlifted to hospital on a neighbouring island when he started to have what sounded like an extreme panic attack. No sooner had they packed up and left than AIR issued a statement to the effect that they would not be working with Duran Duran, at any location anywhere in the world, ever again.

By which I was horrified. My precious charges were now full-blown divas. Word reached me several times a week of drug-fuelled capers gone horribly wrong, some of which turned into life-threatening incidents. There were worrying signs that the charmed planet they inhabited was spinning out of control. They returned to the UK briefly, to support Dire Straits in a fundraiser for the heir to the throne's Prince's Trust. They shook hands with Charles and with Princess Diana, allegedly their biggest fan, which was captured on film and which conferred an unofficial Royal seal of approval. Thanks to which, Duran Duran's stock rose even higher. Unfortunately, they let themselves down at an under-rehearsed Mencap benefit that dissolved into a PR disaster, with no profits recouped for the charity. Yet it no longer seemed to matter when they failed to perform well, ironically. The screaming fans were now so deafening that you couldn't hear the band play anyway. They might as well have been the Beatles.

They completed the third album eventually in Australia, at EMI's own studios there. Nick worked closely with Alex Sadkin, and the result surpassed my breath-holding expectations. *Seven And The Ragged Tiger*, its title a reference to the group's five members plus their managers Paul and Mike Berrow, exuded art-pop aestheticism. It was lush and ornate, to the point of opalescence. It was a bit *too* opalescent, if you asked me. I hadn't been expecting quite so much in the way of textural overload. My initial impression at playback was that the album was the collaborative collage of Rhodes and Sadkin, that the others had enjoyed negligible say, and that guitarist Andy Taylor had as good as been sidelined. Having said that, and despite Andy's complaints, his guitar sounded here and there more rock'n'roll than ever. Andy wasn't the only one who was dismayed by this latest state of affairs. John Taylor, too, was irked by Sadkin's approach and Nick's control-freakery. At one point he vented his anger by smashing up a bathroom. The record had taken too long and had cost too much. It raised a warning flag, that I was among the first to spot. Duran Duran were starting to fragment.

Seven And The Ragged Tiger was a success, but at what cost? One track, 'Take the Dice', had a lyric that yielded the answer. It haunted me. Simon sang disturbingly of newspaper headlines and flashing lights. I knew exactly what he meant. Where 'Hungry Like The Wolf' had presented Duran Duran as hunters, the tables had turned. The band were now the prey. How long before they were eaten whole?

I'd gone grey and had lost sleep over the excesses of the album's recording. I hadn't known the half of it. Their plans for the sleeve and the video shoots brought me out in a rash. A tiger walking on water against a backdrop of snow-capped Himalayas? They were having a laugh. Though they did get a tiger past me in the end. They managed to ship a specially-selected living specimen down to Sydney, and got it to the top of the State Library of New South Wales. Smoke bombs were dropped, the poor creature freaked out, mayhem ensued, and only its eyes would ever make it onto the album sleeve. Which meant that the image could have been shot absolutely anywhere. A photo-library picture could have been purchased. We'd never pacify Animal Rights campaigners today, is the point, and rightly so. The rest of their mad ideas went under my head. *Yes*, they were pan-global pop stars whose lives were a sublime adventure. But they were taking the piss. *Yes*, the album gave us their first UK Number One. Was it worth it?

★

In April 1983, Spandau Ballet topped the charts with their masterpiece 'True'. I knew it was a Number One the first time I heard it. We all did. I felt wistful. What I wouldn't have given to be working with those guys now. One is supposed, I know, to be grateful for what one has, and never look a gift tiger in the mouth. But still. In truth, Duran Duran had become more trouble than they were worth. They seemed to have lost the plot. I was losing it too. I glanced around, and there was Wham! I could have had *them*, too! I could have had Bowie. Back came the Dame, after a hiatus during which we'd all assumed he was gone for good. Here he was again, repackaged for the Eighties and set to give the kids a run for their money.

Looking back, what I remember is that the tiger's appetite was insatiable. The rest is mostly a blur. Shapes and sounds still emerge from the shadows to catch me unawares. I am beckoned back into a world gone by. Its soundtrack was the contagious cacophony of 'New Moon On Monday'; the tom-tom chants and freakery of 'Wild Boys', its million-pound video shot on Pinewood's 007 Stage, landing the Brit Award for British Video of the Year; the relentless stuttering of 'The Reflex' – the song of 1984 and their most successful single ever. The 'Fab Five', as America called them, *did* break The Land of the Free. They *did* make the cover of *Rolling Stone*. They *did* realise their teenage dream, and got to play Madison Square Garden. They *did* have merchandise with their name emblazoned all over it: hats, T-shirts, head bands, tote bags, batteries. Yes. Coca-Cola sponsored their tour, a sign of the corporate times. John's joke at the meeting with the people from Coke – that to be honest, he preferred a nice Pepsi – hinted at anarchy. I liked that. It made me think of the Sex Pistols, then of Frankie Goes to Hollywood, the band I had so stupidly declined to sign. Whenever Duran Duran sought to shake things up, it never felt real.

In 1984, I'd had the band for just four years. A lifetime. They had changed the way I felt about music. They had changed *me*. An insidious chill came over me the day the penny dropped. What about my wife, my children, our new baby on the way? What about the next band, the next hit, the next big thing? The bands, the hits, the big things after that? I needed to stop. To calm down. To catch up on some sleep. Baby, I tried.

24

OPPORTUNITIES

I heard a record called 'West End Girls', by two guys calling themselves the Pet Shop Boys. The singer and wordsmith was Neil Tennant, the bespectacled *Smash Hits* journalist who'd given my Duran boys a lukewarm review three years earlier. His sidekick was a Blackpool-born synth-wizard Architecture student and twelve-inch collector, not a euphemism, by the name of Chris Lowe. Record-sleeve designer and writer Tom Watkins, who was now moving into management and with whom I'd crossed paths, had signed them. I didn't have much time for Tom, despite his considerable reputation. But that didn't matter. I wanted his protégés on EMI.

'West End Girls' had 'hit' written all over it. It was unlike anything I could think of having heard before. Broken glass hadn't sounded like this since Kate Bush smashed some of Abbey Road Studios' canteen cups and saucers on 'Babooshka' with a Fairlight. It even had a keyboard part that recreated a Gregorian chant. Its lyrics were succinct, succulent and poetic, apparently inspired by T.S. Eliot's *The Waste Land*. The track condensed Eighties glamour and social division into the disposable carton of a pop song. It even contained a reference to Russian history. The lyric 'From Lake Geneva to the Finland Station' alluded to the journey made by Vladimir Lenin 'in a sealed carriage'. It was urban desperation to an exquisitely danceable tune. Not only that, but Neil rapped on it. The Pet Shop Boys as English hip hop group? Was I hearing things? He sounded the way rap might have sounded if delivered by Dame Edith Sitwell. The song made me feel how I felt the first time I heard Kate's 'Wuthering Heights', when I first caught the Frankies' 'Relax'. It wasn't even finished. Although as far as I was concerned, this pop poetry to music was perfect just as it was.

It came out on the CBS Epic label, and I thought I'd missed my chance. It conquered the clubs but flopped in the charts. The hit parade wasn't ready for them. When it was, it would embrace them wholeheartedly. This duo would endure.

Journalist Neil was at a crossroads, and was weighing up his options. Now nearly thirty years old, he wanted to leave his job at *Smash Hits* and throw everything he had into a last-ditch bid for pop stardom. But he was cautious. Placing all his eggs in one basket was hardly Neil's style. Even though he and Chris had gone to New York, worked with American record producer Bobby Orlando and released a single, he couldn't quite bring himself to turn his back on his day job. It was too great a risk. So he stayed at *Smash Hits*: all the way to when I signed them to EMI in April 1985.

I could tell from the start that they wouldn't be a pushover. They had their own ideas about how they wanted to sound, how they wanted to look and what they felt they could achieve. But when it came to negotiating contracts and securing budgets for their vast vision, they were happy to take a back seat and defer to Watkins's chutzpah. The combination worked. Neil did all the talking at our meetings, and floored me with his intelligence. They would prefer not to be on EMI itself, if that was ok. They would rather their records be released on the Parlophone imprint. The label that had been more than good enough for Kate Bush and Duran Duran felt somewhat naff to Neil, he said. I laughed my head off. I couldn't help myself. Other than that, they couldn't have been friendlier nor more polite. As purveyors of exquisite taste, as they were in those days, they could be, how can I put this, rather snooty.

They had met by chance, in a Hi-Fi shop on the King's Road close to Neil's small flat above a shoe shop; a store that sold cowboy boots of many colours, to be precise, called R. Soles. They got chatting, and bonded over Bowie. One thing led to another and they started making music together. It wasn't much cop to begin with. Until Chris went home to Blackpool one weekend, sat down at the family piano and composed a piece inspired by Peter Skellern's 1973 hit 'You're a Lady'. Neil conjured a dark lyric to go with it. They called it 'Jealousy'.

It had something, they agreed. What next?

Years later, thanks to me, here they were, signing to Parlophone. They'd amassed a huge catalogue of songs which we were about to take advantage of. I was quietly confident. I knew that 'West End Girls' wasn't a fluke. The tapes they gave me were brimming with great songs. I earmarked one as a future Number One, 'It's a Sin'. Another, called 'Opportunities (Let's Make Lots of Money)' would be their first release on Parlophone.

Produced by the Art of Noise's J.J. Jeczalik, the single took three weeks to record and cost us £70,000. I nearly dropped dead. I nearly did so again when they had it remixed in New York. On first hearing, it sounded like another anthem from the aspirational Eighties. Listen more closely and you could hear clues that all was not quite as it seemed. Intelligent, ironic pop was a new one on me.

I was surprised when 'Opportunities' stiffed down in the hundreds. My instincts and experience had pointed me at a Top Ten hit. Yes, about my Midas touch…

★

A couple of Duran Duran splinter projects distracted me. Andy and John Taylor went to New York to work with Robert Palmer, as part of a supergroup dubbed the Power Station. Nick and Simon diverted to Paris, and immersed themselves in their side project Arcadia. I crossed the channel to check on how they were getting on, and was gobsmacked by what I'd found. If I'd thought them decadent during the good old days, they'd gone beyond reason now. They had taken, not a regular luxury suite each, but an entire floor of their Parisian hotel. Grace Jones, a guest on the album alongside Sting, Herbie Hancock and David Gilmour of Pink Floyd, was a frequent visitor. As was Simon's supermodel fiancée, Yasmin Parvaneh.

It was during my stay that Mick Jagger rocked up one night, looking like a gilded sculpture. I'd seen him before, of course – in restaurants, across state rooms and on international stages down the years – but never point-blank, off-duty, unaccompanied. I could hardly believe my luck! Here was my chance! At last, as one of the most successful A&R men in the land, I was about to sit down in a private hotel suite in one of the most glamorous cities on earth, and commune with one of the world's greatest rock legends. I admit, I was anything but cool. I could barely contain myself. I bounded over, elbowed my way into the conversation he was having, and started to talk. Nineteen to the dozen. Giving it all that. Nobody else could get a syllable in edgeways. Not that I gave a toss. The floor was mine. I had verbal diarrhoea. I hadn't sniffed so much as a pinch of coke, but I was sweating like a side of ham. I had it coming.

'Oh, do fuck off,' said Jagger.

I was thrilled. Until then, the only rock star ever to have told me to fuck off was Paul McCartney.

★

Arcadia proved, in the end, to be nothing but a glorious folly. Profligacy had reached stupendous heights. Nick had bought himself an apartment in Paris, but was still ordering hotel Room Service. He and Simon both dyed their blond hair black, thus rendering themselves almost unrecognisable. The video for Arcadia's first single, 'Election Day', made 'Rio' look like an episode of *EastEnders*. Models cavorted, horse-headed men stripped, they all paraded about admiring the ceilings. This was Luis Buñuel making a Bacardi ad. The director, Roger Christian, had been a production designer on Ridley Scott's 1979 Sci-Fi horror flick *Alien*. They were working with Oscar-winning film-makers now. This is how mad it all was.

I'd heard a few rough mixes of the Arcadia album, and I thought that they sounded terrific. This unashamed vanity project featured some of Nick's and Simon's finest work to date. Liberated from stultifying routine and tyranny, Simon surpassed himself as a lyricist. As a singer, too, he sounded more natural and unforced. I had high hopes for this record… or I might have done, had they stopped mixing it. When at last it saw the light of day, *So Red The Rose* was wilting. Neither album nor single performed in proportion to what we'd spent on them. The critics were once again divided. Where some heard Japan's *Tin Drum* or Bowie's Eno-assisted masterpieces, others smelled rancid Emperor's New Clothes, and crossed the road to avoid the stench.

The Power Station did rather better. 'Some Like It Hot' lived up to its hype. Their cover of Bolan's 'Get it On (Bang a Gong)' was decent, and would have gone down well live. The trouble was, fickle

Robert Palmer quit on the eve of their tour. He had his own album to finish, you see. The twenty-sixth Marquis des Barres, aka Michael Des Barres, replaced him. His infamous wife was the legendary rock groupie Pamela. Would the two halves of Duran Duran ever re-form? Would hell be freezing over any time soon?

Setting many extra-curriculars aside, the boys reconvened in 1985 to record a Bond theme. 'A View To A Kill' was the exceptional result. But a faceless non-star called Paul Hardcastle, with multiple remixes of his track '19,' scuppered their chances of a second UK Number One. The band reassembled for the Philadelphia leg of Live Aid that July. It was the last time we'd see this line-up together on stage for a long time. They were eclipsed that day by another EMI act. The famine fundraiser's finest hour belonged to, and will always be synonymous with, Freddie Mercury.

★

At long last, Terry Slater jumped ship. I confess, I had mixed feelings about his departure. While on the one hand I was delighted to see the back of him, on the other I was nervous about running the show by myself. Why did he quit? He suddenly found himself with bigger fish to fry. He'd signed on as manager of Norwegian pop sensations A-ha, whose single 'Take on Me' was shredding the charts.

At about the same time I was introduced to Belouis Some by the Durans' managers Mike and Paul Berrow. He had started life as Neville Keighley in South London's Forest Hill. 'Neville' being not much of a pop-star name, he'd started toying with ideas for a replacement, and had settled on the first name Louis. Legend has it that his girlfriend said, 'Catchy name, but it would be better if you could be Louis Something.' He reinvented himself as Belouis Some. His 'Imagination' single cost me about £25,000. There was remix after remix, but we got it right in the end, hitting the Top Twenty in February 1986. Sometimes you hear a hit in the elementary material, but know that it is going to need work. It was extremely satisfying, some while later, to find myself passing a fairground and hearing 'Imagination' blasting out over the dodgems.

I remained confident about the remake of the Pet Shop Boys' 'West End Girls'. It now had a slower pace and a rounder sound.

Fresh touches like sampled street noise and brass fleshed it into a full widescreen production. The Pet Shop Boys owned the first few months of 1986, and were rewarded with a Number One hit. They released *Please*, their debut album. It went platinum in the UK, the US and elsewhere, shifting three million copies.

Malcolm McLaren had reared his ugly head again, in the guise of the pop star he had always longed to be. He was the wrong side of forty. Despite which, his 'Buffalo Gals' and 'Madame Butterfly' did rather well. Trevor Horn, 'the man who invented the Eighties,' produced his quaint, now re-released album, *Duck Rock*.

The ghosts of the past had been banished. EMI was in good shape. Which was boring. Ten years had elapsed since the Sex Pistols took on the Establishment, all but wrecked our record company, tidal-waved the media and almost won. Things had turned a bit safe since their cataclysmic coming and shameful departure. High time, thought I, for another dose of bad taste.

25

BURN, BABY, BURN

Sigue Sigue Sputnik's name was a phrase used by gang members on the streets of Moscow. It meant 'Burn, burn satellite', and that's precisely what this bunch intended to do. Having evolved from the ashes of punk and the New Romantics, they were looking to do something incendiary of their own. Their sound was a blend of the riffs of Elvis and Eddie Cochran and the attitude of the Sex Pistols, filtered through sequencers. They looked and sounded like an electric shock: bleached barnets, pink pineapple hairdos, codpieces, fishnet facewear, kinky stiletto boots. In a nutshell, rock panto. Oh yes it was.

I had to have them. Some of my colleagues at EMI thought I'd finally lost the plot. At one early meeting about the band, the Promotions team were so incensed that I'd signed such 'trash' to the label, every one of them walked out in protest.

Tony James, former Generation X bassist and their leader, wanted David Bowie to produce them. I picked myself up off the floor, laughed them down the pub, and got them to settle for Giorgio Moroder. I was forced to eat my own mirth years later when Bowie turned round and covered their first single and biggest hit, 'Love Missile F1-11'. Their publicist was Magenta De Vine, the glass-eyed temptress who presented TV's *Network 7*. She and Tony were an item for a while, before he lost his heart to the queen of 'Yoof' telly, Janet Street-Porter. Work that one out.

Anyway, so far, so good. The band were soon all over *The Sun* newspaper, boasting about their million-pound record deal. Believe me, it was less than half that: I was the one who wrote the cheque. Not that I cared. Hype was their middle name. Not only was it part of their masterplan, it was the point of them.

With its refrain of 'Shoot it up!' and its crass self-mockery, 'Love Missile F1-11' was nothing if not nuke-rock. Released in February 1986, it took off like a rocket, zoomed to Number Three in the UK and was a massive hit across Europe and Asia. Off they went to *Top Of The Pops*, where they didn't behave like bastards. Tony and lead singer Martin Degville appeared on television breakfast show *TV-am*, causing presenter Ann Diamond's pretty jaw to drop. It was too early in the day for that kind of thing. The single owed at least part of its success to its inclusion in that year's teen-comedy sensation, *Ferris Bueller's Day Off*, starring Matthew Broderick.

There would be six Sigue Sigue singles for EMI. '21st Century Boy' was the follow-up, which failed to convince the critics but still went Top Twenty, pursued by the album, *Flaunt It*. That went Top Ten, in spite of scathing reviews. The band treated the silent pauses between the tracks of their record like the back of a magazine. To them, this was glaringly obvious advertising space. *i-D* magazine and Studio Line from L'Oréal fell for it, and bought twenty-to-thirty-second slots. Plenty were left over, allowing the group to create spoof ads of their own. When asked to explain, Tony James responded in haughty style. 'Commercialism is rampant in society,' he pronounced. 'Maybe we're a little more honest than some groups I could mention.'

Thus did they take the pop-art jape to a whole new level in the branding-obsessed 1980s. It was hilarious. I was thrilled to be part of the hoax. To begin with, at least.

It became apparent all too soon that Sigue Sigue Sputnik were sporting those less than comfortable Emperor's New Clothes. They were not, after all, a proper band. There was no musical ethos nor mission. They really were just hype. About that: while it's true that it can propel you all the way to superstardom, no way can it keep you there. Only talent, commitment and luck can do that. There was no magic here, nor even a whiff of mystique. The only smell that I could detect was cynicism. They were a con, and they were soon found out. Their gigs were poorly attended. Those who came, left unmoved. Singer Martin took to lashing out, causing violence to erupt in the gangways.

They soldiered on. I'm not sure we wanted them to. EMI, and that included me, had had enough of them by then. Two years elapsed before they tried again with a second album. *Dressed for Excess* was produced by Stock, Aitken and Waterman, which said it all. The con artists had compromised the musical integrity they never had. The album peaked in the UK at Number Fifty-Three. It sold an awful lot of copies in Brazil.

I was at least spared humiliation around the boardroom table at Manchester Square. I was gone by then. I was five and a half thousand miles away in Los Angeles, where someone new was making me an offer I couldn't refuse.

★

When my plane landed in LAX, I was met by a chauffeur. He conveyed me in a flash limo to Universal City, where I was presented to the legendary Irving Azoff. Irving had recently been appointed head of the label which had enjoyed huge success down the years with Elton John, Neil Diamond, the Who, Cher, Lynyrd Skynyrd and Olivia Newton-John, and had cleaned up with the soundtrack of the 1973 Oscar-winner *The Sting*. During the 1970s and 1980s, MCA reissued a huge number of classic rock'n'roll recordings made by artists who had once belonged to labels later absorbed by MCA, including 'Rock Around the Clock' by Bill Haley & His Comets. He was infamous not least for having stolen the Eagles from his arch-rival David Geffen. He wanted me as MD of MCA UK, the British arm of the label. Let me think: silly not to. I floated back to London on a nebula of nines, and went straight to the company's Brewer Street offices. Bigger role, bigger office, bigger expenses, *much* bigger pay. Yeah, baby.

We started well, with Kim Wilde's hi-energy cover of the Supremes' 'You Keep Me Hanging On'. Which was a massive hit, here, there and everywhere. We had Wendy James, sexy frontress of pop-punk outfit Transvision Vamp. Their first single, 'Revolution Baby', was released in December 1986 stalled at Number Seventy-Seven. The second, a cover of Holly and the Italians' 'Tell That Girl to Shut Up', didn't fare much better. It was third time lucky with 'I Want Your Love', an international breakthrough. I was all set to transform Wendy into the British Madonna.

I'd barely even got started when Irving Azoff resigned from MCA to launch his own label, Giant Records, and the MCA's operation in the UK was shut down. We the staff were all fired overnight. Rumours of connections to organised crime circulated for years. There was even a book about it, called *Stiffed: A True Story of MCA, The Music Business, and The Mafia* by William Knoedelseder, a business writer for the *Los Angeles Times*. I read it. I was none the wiser.

★

Needs must. Tail between legs, stiff upper lip. I went back to A&R, this time for London Records: a dance-pop label who were in need of a few rock acts. But I was up against Pete Tong, the star DJ who dominated the place. We did sign Happy Mondays, and put on a lavish banquet for the group in an Italian restaurant in Fulham. When singer Shaun Ryder wound up face-down in the food, I knew that the band had seen better days and that it would be to my cost.

Once again, the industry was changing. For the first time in my career, I felt adrift. I was an anachronism. I was old-school. I was a fish out of water during what they were calling the dance era. The charts were brimming with dance acts, one- or two-hit wonders made by anonymous anti-stars who loathed 'the business'. No sooner had I departed than the label signed a tough boy band called East 17. They were pipped at the post when they tried to sign a promising new girl group. The bidding war to end bidding wars did not go London's way. The Spice Girls signed to Virgin.

What goes around, comes around. Virgin merged with EMI. I found myself back there, minus my Midas touch. I failed to sign any of the Brit-pop acts I pursued, including Suede, Blur and Oasis. Each band slipped noticeably through my fingers. I'd had my day, clearly. Never go back.

There was one last hurrah for me in A&R, at the Sanctuary label. I was head-hunted again, and was offered my own imprint, Planet-3. I left their Kensington Olympia offices the day I signed the contract giving thanks for this much-needed golden reprieve. I notched up a modest hit with an MCA reject, the alternative rock band Intastella, who together with post-Mondays Shaun Ryder gave us *Drifter*. My biggest success for the label was in 1995 with 'Love City Groove' by the band of the same name, who provided us with our very own

Song for Europe. It had come to this. Despite the fact that we were the bookmakers' choice as runaway winners at the Point Theatre Dublin, the curse of Eurovision had struck again. We limped in tenth. Norwegian group Secret Garden took the trophy, with their song 'Nocturne'. Which wasn't even a song, FYI. By anybody's standards, their entry was an instrumental with some afterthought vocals. Is this sounding like sour grapes? My consolation prize was a single that made it to a respectable Number Seven. I was thankful for small mercies.

★

On 26th October 2010, my life in music rewound in a heartbeat one evening when I spotted Ray Davies across the tables at the Brits. He was being honoured with a Lifetime Achievement Award that night, and I couldn't help feeling proud. Since I'd last seen him, Ray, the so-called Quiet One, had married three times, fallen out with his brother Dave, killed the Kinks, attempted suicide by drug overdose, fallen in love with the Pretenders' Chrissie Hynde and had a daughter with her, had been shot in the leg in New Orleans by a thief who had snatched his companion's handbag, and was very lucky indeed to be alive. He was a father of four, and he looked it. After years of struggling, juggling record companies and facing the shame of dwindling record sales he had become, through no fault of his own, the undisputed godfather of Britpop. I didn't rush over to greet my long-lost friend. What was the point? What would we say to each other?

That unexpected glimpse of Ray cast my mind back further, all the way to Pete Bardens. The precious partner in crime of my misspent youth had gone to California, just as Brian Auger had done. Restless Pete remained a musical force, playing with Camel, the Prog Rock group he co-founded, as well as all those other acts. He was diagnosed with a brain tumour in 2001. Typical Pete, he refused to lie down and give in to it. He celebrated instead, staging a summer concert that turned out to be his last, with special guests Sheila E., Ben Harper and a trio of old-time pals: John Mayall, John McVie and Mick Fleetwood. He died of lung cancer in Malibu in January 2002, aged only fifty-seven. His double CD *Write My Name In The Dust: The Anthology 1963-2002* is one of my most treasured possessions.

189

I remembered the day I walked into that empty ballet hall on Latimer Road and came face to face with a genius: a smiling genius with long hair, called Pete, thrashing blues piano as though his young life depended on it. He changed my own in so many ways. I never got to thank him. It was the same with Mum and Dad. I had lost them both and I had many regrets, not least that I'd never told them how much I loved them. We think there is time. We think we'll get round to things. But time slips and slides. It spends itself behind our backs. It does its own thing, quietly, waiting for no one. We miss it when it's gone.

★

As for the music industry: it evaporated. Sanctuary enjoyed a boom, then a terminal slump. EMI was lost to Terra Firma. People stopped buying physical music and turned to downloads. All those prophets who'd been ridiculed for foretelling the digital revolution had obviously been right all along.

...EXHALE

Does the A&R man matter today? He still does. Technology has changed his game, and has diminished his expense account. But he lives, he breathes. He or she must still know their stuff. The right producer has to be hired, a good enough recording studio has to be found, and everything still has to be brought in under budget. The pressure to score hits has never waned. Hits are where it's at, they are the Holy Grail, especially to the major record companies. The most valuable artist is the one who can write his own songs. Covers were all too common, way back when. Carefully-chosen, they had the potential to become huge hits, and often were. But a band or artist who can write their own is always going to last much longer. Chasing around for great songs to cover, which is basically what Simon Cowell does at his label Syco, is an unconscionable slog and not exactly creative.

Perhaps the greatest irony of all is that technology has returned us to the age of the single. Music fans can now select individual songs by a favourite artist or a new discovery they want to check out, via the various means available on the internet: Amazon, Spotify, Google Play Music, YouTube, Napster, Tidal, Apple Music and so on. They can now buy only the tracks they like, and don't have to bother investing in the whole album. Hence, the demise of the album. Hence, significantly reduced income for the artist and the record company. Bands have no choice these days, they have to tour whether they like it or not. Along with merchandising, live performing has become their primary source of income. Record companies now take their percentage from merchandising and publishing, aka songwriting. It's the only way to ensure that they will make any money. It is also the reason why so many old-school record companies have vanished without trace. Incidentally, when you purchase a download, you are automatically contributing to PPL and PRS – Public Performance Licence and the Performing Rights Society, and MCPS – the Mechanical Copyright Protection Society – as well as to royalties for the artist and the server. The main reason that the internet has taken over, in my opinion, is speed. You hear a song on the radio, you download it from iTunes. No pre-ordering, no queueing, no wait. You want it, you've got it. It works.

Oh, those quaint old, good old days. The way we once did things seems medieval now. We took one single, got it into the UK charts, got it onto the BBC Radio 1 playlist and subsequently onto the indie playlists, of which there were about a hundred. So yes, underhand methods were deployed. They got results. We'd be fined heavily if we got caught hyping a record, but everyone did it. It was a risk worth taking: the international record companies watched the UK charts like hawks, and took the successful bands on for their territories. We would follow up with a second single and an album release, then send the band on tour supporting a major act. The cost incurred was astronomical, not least for the buy-on: which is when the record company has to pay a star band for the privilege of its band opening for them on the road. Factor in the support personnel, the hotels, the trucks, the travel expenses and you begin to get the picture. Advances remain recoupable. But nowadays, record companies take a cut from merchandising sales as well as record sales. Royalties are a fraction of what they once were. Most artists supplement their incomes, in addition to the live gigs and the merchandise, by tying up syncs with advertising and films, now a huge aspect of the industry.

Hype still happens. I am employed today as a lecturer on the music business, based at City, University of London. My students there are across it. It might be via mobile and iPad now, but technology hasn't eliminated it. The new media are able to promote the kind of songs which would not, in the past, have received blanket airplay. Thus, an individual who shares a favourite song by phone with his friends can boost sales considerably, unwittingly or otherwise. Viral marketing is the name of today's game. It's a far cry from when BBC Radio 1 was the most important tool in our box. The station still matters, but nowhere near as much. CD sales dropped like a stone with the emergence of the new media. Now Spotify, to name but one, has its own playlists, compiled via downloads. As for promotion, what could be simpler? Your artist can record himself on a laptop in his bedroom. You book a string of club dates around the country, he does his PAs, a couple of songs a night. You make friends, network the audiences, the manager gets to know the fans, and a fanbase is born. The fans download your songs, they share them, and you're out there.

★

I never imagined myself saying this: that I remember with fondness those tedious monthly forecast meetings, based on singles sales. You had your artist, and you decided at this meeting how many of their albums would be pressed. With a big-name act, we'd have to be ready, as we'd expect the album to go straight to Number One. I cringe to recall a particular incident during the Eighties when a label that should remain nameless had two hundred and fifty thousand albums pre-ordered on the strength of the sales of the previous single. All quarter of a million albums had to be melted down. This is never going to happen with the internet. Costs of sales are virtually zero. There is no stockpiling.

The demise of the album is a tragedy, as far as I'm concerned. I'd whip us all back to the age of vinyl if I could. I have appreciated its revived popularity in recent years. I adore LP covers: they contain so much great information. But no-one in their right mind could regard vinyl today as anything other than a niche product. It has had its day, and that is that. It is never going to overcome technology. Neither am I, dear reader. Neither am I.

But there is plenty for which to be thankful. The love of my life is still my wife. Angie and I made good children, and they have made wonderful lives for themselves. Kate is creative producer for visitor programmes and exhibitions at Kew Gardens; Barney works for the National Archives; and Rory, a former tree surgeon at Kew, is now reisdent Arborist the National Trust-owned Arboretum in Dyffryn, Wales.

I may be an ex-A&R man who failed to become a rock star. I never got to be Pablo Picasso or David Hockney either. But I can still play. I can still paint. I can still dream.

APPENDIX

I am often asked about the guitars I have owned, played and loved. Perhaps they owned, played and loved me in return. The relationship between a musician and his instrument is a curious and magical thing. I think of Queen's Brian May and his Red Special, hand-crafted lovingly by him and his father from the wooden surround of an old domestic fireplace; of Paul McCartney, and the precious Höfner bass he has owned and played since the earliest days of the Beatles; of the Ox, and the Status Graphite Buzzard Bass that was designed specially for him in later days; and of Led Zeppelin's John Paul Jones and his Fender Bass V, which he called 'the ugliest bass guitar in the world.'

Here, for the record, is a run-down of the guitars I have been proud to call my own, and which have been such an important part of my life:

My first guitar: a Spanish guitar bought for me by my father when I was eleven.

My second: a six-string Dallas, bought in Purley, on which I played Shadows and Duane Eddy numbers in front of the school.

My third: I wanted to be like Paul McCartney, and to play a bass guitar like his, but I couldn't afford a Höfner. I did get one with a violin-shaped body, though: not a well-known brand, I just fell in love with the shape.

My fourth: I got a good bass, at last: a Gibson EB-O in red cherry, which I played while in Shotgun Express.

My fifth: A Gibson EB3. I played it on all the sessions, including on Kim Fowley's cover of 'They're Coming to Take Me Away, Ha Haaa!'

My sixth: With my Advance from Atlantic, I bought a six-string Fender bass. I played it on the Trinity's *Streetnoise* album.

My seventh: A Fender jazz bass, which I played while with King Crimson and Arthur Brown.

★

Lost for forty years, *Dave Ambrose's Dark Nebula* is now available on Spotify and YouTube.

INDEX

Q-Tips (band), 152
Quaife, Pete, 53
Quarry Men, the (skiffle group), 24
Queen (band)
    backstage cavortings, 5
    at EMI, 138, 158–9
    pull out of *Today* show, 145–6
    Roof Gardens party (1986), 159
    'Bohemian Rhapsody', 138

R. Soles (King's Road shoe shop), 180
racial prejudice and race riots (1958),
    39
Radio Caroline, 52
Radio Luxembourg, 19, 20, 23
Ram Jam Club, Brixton, 85
Ramones, 142
Ramrods (band), 53
Ravensbourne University London, 54
Ray Davies Quartet, 53, 89
Redding, Noel, 96, 97
Redding, Otis, 81
Reed, Lou, 'Walk on the Wild Side', 4
Reigate, 12, 25, 27, 45–6
Reigate County School for Girls, 17
Relf, Keith, 97
Rhodes, Nick
    in DA's fantasy supergroup, 1
    in Duran Duran, 162, 170, 176–7
    and Kajagoogoo, 173–4
    Arcadia side project, 181, 182
Richard, Cliff, 146
    'Move It', 23
Richards, Keith, 20, 50, 54, 147
Richardson, J.P. (The Big Bopper), 42
Roaring Twenties, The (Soho
    nightclub), 59
Robert Stigwood Organisation
    (record label), 81
Robinson, Tom, 152
rock and pop stardom
    advice on 'making it', 2–4, 8
    downside, 2
    in MeToo era, 5–6
    and sex, 4–7
    and style and fashion, 3, 163–4

Rock and Roll Hall of Fame, 121
'Rock Island Line', 23–4
rock 'n' roll
    beginnings in America, 21
    and teen culture, 22, 43
    arrives in Britain, 19–21
    British first wave, 22–3
    skiffle craze, 23–4
    in late 1950s and early '60s, 42, 43
    British R&B scene, 49–52, 53
    pub rock, 129, 138
    Glam rock, 138, 163
    punk rock, 3, 142, 145
    metal rock, 174
Rolling Stone (magazine), 52, 117, 178
Rolling Stones
    formation, 50
    first gig, 23
    at the Scene Club, 52
    at the Flamingo, 81
    touring, 71
    sign with EMI, 147
    'Honky Tonk Women', 40, 64
    'Jumpin' Jack Flash', 116
    'Satisfaction', 97
Rollins, Len, 86–7, 88, 91
Rollins, Sue (DA's first wife)
    DA first meets, 86–7
    early relationship, 87–8
    wedding, 91
    married life, 91, 95, 98, 105, 108–9,
        117, 124
    opposes DA joining Fleetwood
        Mac, 101
    moves to House of Wax, 124–5
    waitress, 125
    breakdown of marriage, 125, 129,
        131–2, 132–3
    takes live-in lover, 131–2
    divorce, 134
    in later life, 134
Ronettes, 43, 71
Ronnie Scott's Jazz Club, 51, 102
Ronson, Mick, 141
Roof Gardens party (1986), 159
Ross, Diana, 169
Rotten, Johnny *see* Lydon, John